TED ANDERSON AND

NIPPON'S GUEST

A Sailor POW in Japan

1995

Published by
Devonshire House
Christow
Devon EX6 7LU

© Copyright Robin Rowe 1995

ISBN 0-9524513-2-8

British Library Cataloguing in Publication Data
A catalogue record for this book
is available from the British Library

Printed and Bound in Great Britain by
Abbot Litho Press Ltd

NIPPON'S GUEST

Inset Photo: Ted Anderson in 1939
Cover Design: RJR

Edward John Anderson, junior and senior. (Anderson)

Contents

Illustrations

Foreword

Nippon's Guest is the true story of a prisoner of war in Japanese hands based on two accounts written by Chief Mechanician Ted Anderson. The first is the unpublished diaries he kept for three and a half years while in captivity and the other is an unedited typescript of about 80,000 words that he wrote from the diaries and memory in the 1970s.

This book is a shortened mixture of both, using the diary to give chronological order and the typescript for anecdotal and descriptive narrative. There have been some necessary editorial alterations and explanatory notes have been added; but apart from these the story is in Ted's own words.

The diary entries are in quotation marks and preceded by a date to distinguish them from the narrative text. With the exception of the first chapter, which contains additional material, the notes are in italics.

I would like to thank Mrs Thyra Anderson and her family for allowing me the timely opportunity of working on and publishing her late husband's diaries and subsequent manuscripts to mark the fiftieth anniversary of VJ-Day, 15th August 1945.

Robin Rowe
Christow 1995

CHAPTER 1

The Last Days of HMS Exeter

'Sunday 29th March 1942, at Macassar in the Celebes, Dutch E. Indies.

'Today marks the 1st month since the *Exeter* engaged the enemy for the last time and our incarceration as prisoners of war. In retrospect the month presents a most grotesque and confused picture. By Friday 27th [February] when we first engaged Japanese naval forces we were utterly frayed by constant air attack both in and out of harbour.'

These were the opening words of a diary started by Edward John Anderson in the prisoner of war camp at Macassar in the Celebes. A journal he was to keep on any scraps of paper he could beg, borrow or steal right up to 1945 when, employed by the Japanese as a road sweeper near Nagasaki, he was to witness the event that ended World War II and his captivity; the detonation of the world's third atomic bomb.

Like other diarists, particularly those in captivity, he wrote in a simple code—in fact Pitman's shorthand—subsequently transcribing it into a full-length manuscript. The diary itself was used as evidence in the subsequent war crimes trials of his captors.

Edward, or Ted as he was more usually known, was born on 30th October 1911 at 39 Sithney Street, St Budeaux, Plymouth. His father, Edward John senior, was a Chief Petty Officer Cook in the Royal Navy who at one time had the distinction of being the champion breadmaker of the Mediterranean fleet. He and Edith his wife, brought their son and daughter up with a respect for tradition and authority and probably, as with most naval families, an appreciation of the value of an underlying routine with which to order one's life; a concept that was in later years to stand Ted and his fellow prisoners in good stead. Raised in this fashion it ought not to be surprising that Ted joined the Royal Navy but that was not his original intention, because in 1927 at the age of fifteen he decided on a career in engineering and took up an apprenticeship in Devonport dockyard. Then fate in the shape of the depression took a hand for, having served his five years, on the day he completed his apprenticeship, he received a small slip of paper entitled:

D.—487 (Revised—April 1926) <u>**Notice of Discharge**</u>

It informed him that the services of: 'Man's name: 11116 Wanderson (sic), Grade or Class: Hired Founder' would not be required after Monday the 28th November 1932 in consequence of 'adjustment of trades'. A message that has a familiar ring about it in naval dockyards today.

The early nineteen thirties were bad years in which to be made redundant with massive unemployment countrywide. There was no pay-off or redundancy money in those days, the dockyard had no other job for him and there was little hope for him in the Plymouth area. To make matters worse Edward senior, having left the Royal Navy—albeit temporarily until recalled in 1939—was out of work and with little money coming in, the family could not afford another mouth to feed. On the face of it there seemed little choice but to join the lengthening dole queue with his father. But when Ted arrived home that evening he had settled his future and before they even knew he was out of work he announced to his startled parents,

'I've joined the Royal Navy!'

He was lucky to get in because the seamanship branch of the Royal Navy was if anything overmanned and even with the services having perforce taken a cut in pay there was no rush to get back into jobless 'civvy street'. But skilled men were still needed in the engine room department and his five years in the dockyard paid dividends. The realisation that it was only due to his training that he was able to find work influenced Ted for the rest of his life and from then on he became consumed with the desire to increase his knowledge and skills in anything that he could turn his hand or mind to. Amongst other things he taught himself Pitman's shorthand, which seems on the face of it an odd skill to acquire but, as it turned out one of the most useful he could have learned. And so in 1932 he began his new life and, being conscientious and hard working he soon started on the promotion ladder to Chief Petty Officer Mechanician 1st Class, whose engineering skills led by odd twists of fate to the job of road sweeper at Koyaki Jima, Nagasaki.

'Unfortunately I did not see much of the war but my short experience of it was so exciting that at one time I wondered how much longer I could have borne the nerve-wracking ordeal of facing the terrible conditions imposed upon my shipmates and myself in the war at sea. I joined HMS *Exeter* after losing two ships in the initial stages of the war'.

The first ship he 'lost' was HMS *Curlew,* a sloop which on 26th May 1940 was sunk off Norway after being bombed for five days and nights. After swimming for his life a second time (ship unknown) Ted was actually given a choice between the cruiser *Exeter* and the aircraft carrier *Illustrious.* Both were Plymouth manned ships but being a 'little ships' man and probably not much caring for the stricter regime of a big ship, he opted for the cruiser.

'She [*Exeter*] re-commissioned after the famous morale boosting victory over the *Graf Spee* in company with the cruisers *Ajax* and *Achilles.*'

This was when he joined her in his home town, where in Devonport dockyard she had been repaired after her epic battle. On 24 March *Exeter* and her crew steamed out of Plymouth Sound leaving behind their families in a city still smoking from a baptism of bombs that was to continue; making Plymouth the heaviest bombed city in Britain outside of London. A fact that perhaps fortunately the ship's company were not to realise until after their own ordeal was ended.

After a working up period one of *Exeter's* first duties was the patrolling of the North Sea.

'—an icy assignment among the pack-ice which used to strike the ship's sides like giant hammers. On one occasion we shadowed the *Bismarck*. Later the ship was diverted to convoy duties in much more congenial waters.'

Exeter was on convoy duty during the *Bismarck* episode and, although not realised at the time, she was the nearest British warship to *Bismarck* when contact with the enemy was lost and regained. The convoy they were escorting consisted of troopships bound for the 'more congenial waters' of the Indian Ocean where *Exeter* took part in other convoy duties from the Cape of Good Hope to Aden and Ceylon as part of the East Indies Fleet.

This work continued with minor variations until the congeniality ended with Japan entering the war by attacking Pearl Harbour on 7th December and, among other things, landing troops on the eastern coast of Malaya on the 8th. (Curiously the latter event took place in real time some forty minutes before Pearl Harbour due to the eccentricities caused by the International Dateline).

Exeter was ordered to join Admiral Tom Phillips's Force Z, consisting of the battle-cruiser *Repulse* and the battleship *Prince of Wales* who were then on their way to attack the Japanese invasion forces off Malaya. Eager for action with the big ships, *Exeter*'s skipper, Captain Oliver Gordon, increased speed to 26 knots and headed towards the Malacca Straits. Perhaps fortunately for *Exeter* and her crew he was unable to catch up with Admiral Phillips because only hours after, *Prince of Wales, Repulse* and the Admiral himself were at the bottom of the South China Sea.

Reinforcements for Malaya and Singapore became the next priority and *Exeter*'s task was to escort troop convoys from Ceylon to the Banka Straits, in the East Indies, together with the old D-class cruisers *Danae, Dragon* and *Durban.* The convoys were then taken over by the Australian cruiser *Hobart* for the final run to Singapore. As the convoys were timed to arrive at their destination during the hours of darkness it followed that *Exeter*'s leg was carried out in daylight and presumably, at much the same time of day. It was therefore an easy task for the numerous patrolling Japanese floatplanes to report their movements and inform the bombers that had unhindered domination of the air.

With desperate weariness the ships battled on into February and Ted wrote a month later in his diary:

'—Here she was engaged on convoy work between Singapore and Batavia (now Djakarta) in Java. At one time we played rugger against a team from the destroyer *Jupiter* whilst there was an air raid on the town. As we walked back to the ship there were long lines of Spitfires drawn up beside the road. It seemed we were about to get the air support we so badly needed.'

The fighters Ted saw along the road were in fact fifty Hurricanes brought from Port Sudan to Batavia on 27 January by the aircraft carrier *Indomitable.* The air support Ted hoped for did not materialise. Time and again in the opening stages of the Far East war Japanese planes were to destroy their British and American adversaries while they were conveniently lined up in rows on their airfields. Within forty-eight hours of their arrival all the Hurricanes had been destroyed, mostly on the ground.

'During the run between Batavia and Singapore we were sorely harassed by Japanese bombers who used to wait for us to enter the Banka Straits where there was little room for manoeuvre. Daily they indulged in their tormenting play with our gunners, always keeping out of range and tempting them to waste ammunition. Despite their efforts the Japs were thwarted by our captain and the

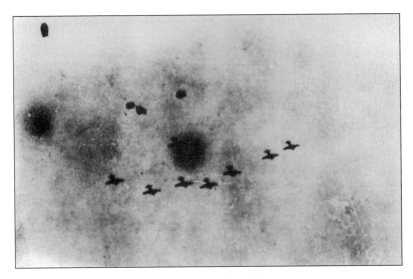

Japanese bombers overhead. (Anderson)

Exeter's AA guns engage the enemy. (Anderson)

navigating officer who seemed to sense where the bombs would fall as soon as they left the plane although near misses and straddles caused terrific reverberations throughout the ship.'

Ted wryly notes that:

'Eventually the Batavia—Singapore run became highly unpopular with the ship's company.'

With the fall of Singapore on 15 February, which came as no surprise to *Exeter*'s men, the Japanese continued their advances and on 25 February two large invasion forces were reported approaching Java. *Exeter*, together with the Australian cruiser *Perth* and the destroyers *Jupiter, Encounter* and *Electra* joined a force of allied ships (part of a naval force called ABDAFLOAT from the initials of the participating nations) under Dutch Admiral Doorman to defend the eastern end of the island. Almost immediately they were at sea searching for the invasion fleet but apart from the inevitable air attack nothing was sighted.

But the following day a patrol aircraft found the enemy and, flying the signal 'Follow me. The enemy is ninety miles away', Admiral Doorman's flagship *de Ruyter* prepared for battle, with the destroyers *Electra, Encounter* and *Jupiter* leading in line abreast followed by *de Ruyter, Exeter, Perth* and *Java*; the American destroyers *John D. Edwards, Paul Jones, John D. Ford* and *Alden* and the Dutch destroyers *Evertsen, Witte de With* and *Kortenaer* on the port flank. Visual contact was made with the enemy at 1605.

It was not as was hoped, the troop transports that they had sighted but the Japanese warships covering the invasion. Nor was the contest to be on equal terms, as the covering force consisted of the heavy cruisers *Nachi* and *Haguro,* the light cruisers *Naka* and *Jintsu* and thirteen modern destroyers. They were also in the advantageous position of being able to bring all their guns to bear as they passed across the bows of the leading ships whilst the allied ships could only fire their forward guns. It was the classic manoeuvre of 'crossing the enemy's T'.

Ted's account continues:

'As I was off watch my action station was at a flooding cabinet the purpose of which was to flood 'A' magazine [in the event of fire] should the need ever arise. This was a duty I hoped that I would never be ordered to perform. The thought of men trapped in the magazine and a torrent of water overwhelming them often intruded itself into my dreams. With me in the same area was the forward fire party and together we crouched against the barbette of 'A' turret trusting that any shells directed against us would hit the other side of the ship. But nevertheless there was a feeling of confidence as the opportunity to match ourselves against Japanese ships had arrived.

'At about 1615 *Exeter* opened fire at a range of 28,000 yards. The concussion of our guns quickly reduced the [nearby] stoker's messdeck to a shambles. Everything loose was flung to the deck. Lamp shades were shattered and much of the lighting was extinguished. Tea urns emptied their contents and a brown flood of tea surged from side to side with the motion of the ship.'

As they approached the enemy, the smaller ships, including the three British destroyers in the van were out of range and had to endure the rain of 8 and 5.5 inch shells from the Japanese cruisers without being able to reply. *Exeter,* limited to her forward turrets and *Houston,* with her fire-power reduced to six guns due to damage sustained earlier, were the only ships able to fire. Despite the heavy shelling and a massed torpedo attack carried out by the Japanese destroyers only *de Ruyter* was hit by a shell which did slight damage, whilst the torpedoes missed altogether. But in the next stage, with the Allied ships drawing near the invasion transports, the action intensified and *Exeter* was hit in the starboard side with an 8 inch shell.

'Suddenly the ship lurched violently; we had been hit. Immediately the ventilating fans ceased their hum and the lighting dimmed almost to extinguishing point. Later we learnt that a Japanese shell had demolished S2 high angle gun and its crew, continuing its passage through the fan flat and an armoured deck to the inboard wing of a boiler in 'B' boiler room [where it exploded]. This misfortune greatly reduced our power as a number of boilers were put out of action and our speed was reduced to six knots. We were in dire peril as two enemy ships closed for the kill. The American cruiser *Houston* came to our aid and took their fire.'

With this reduction in speed Captain Gordon was unable to maintain station and so turned *Exeter* out of line to port. Not knowing the reason for *Exeter*'s turn the ships astern also turned and followed her, leaving *de Ruyter* in isolation. Fortunately the Japanese thought this was some brilliant move to counter the torpedo attack and paused to reconsider the situation, which gave Admiral Doorman time to get his flagship out of danger. Then Captain Waller of the *Perth,* realising *Exeter*'s predicament pulled out to starboard and laid a smoke screen to shield the crippled ship. Meanwhile *Electra*, seeing that the Jap destroyers were preparing to launch another torpedo attack against *Exeter*, steamed at full speed towards them. This gallant destroyer—who had earlier escorted the doomed *Prince of Wales* and *Repulse* and picked up their survivors—was badly mauled by the Japanese cruisers and, reduced to a burning wreck, she sank. To add to the mounting toll of disaster the Dutch destroyer *Kortenaer* was hit and sunk by a torpedo almost immediately afterwards.

With night falling, *Exeter* was unable to take further part in the action and she was ordered to proceed to Sourabaya. Meanwhile Admiral Doorman still wanting to get in among the troop transports, sent the American destroyers in to attack with torpedoes whilst he broke off the engagement with the warships. The Americans however launched their torpedoes well out of range thus making no contribution to the battle and, as there was little more they could do Admiral Doorman also sent them back to Sourabaya to await further orders. In the event they were the only ships of that command still afloat a day later.

Having disengaged from the enemy, Admiral Doorman turned westward through an area of shoals off the Java coast where unknown to him, there happened to be a Dutch minefield. All the ships got through except for the British destroyer *Jupiter* which hit a mine and with a vast explosion, went to the bottom. As the ships turned north to get away from the mines they passed the spot where the *Kortenaer* had sunk, and so *Encounter* stopped to pick up survivors.

Once again the Japanese cruisers with the aid of their floatplanes found and engaged the fleet and in a torpedo attack both *de Ruyter* and *Java* were hit. With fires raging uncontrolled and dead in the water both ships lit up the night sky until they sank.

Admiral Doorman went down with his flagship and Captain Waller of the *Perth* now became senior officer. But with the *Encounter* having already been sent back to Sourabaya and his 'fleet' consisting of his own ship and *Houston*—the latter desperately short of ammunition as well as guns—he too returned to port.

To go back to *Exeter*; Ted takes up his story.

'We made our escape [away from the action and escorted by the Dutch destroyer *Witte de With*] under cover of a heavy smoke screen, on the orders of the Dutch admiral who was in command, arriving at Sourabaya in the first watch [from 8 to midnight]; which was excellent headway considering that there were only two boilers available.

'On arrival it was discovered that the whole of the watch in 'B' boiler room had been killed apart from Stoker Petty Officer Kirkham who escaped miraculously, although he was severely scalded.

'The ship lay all night alongside the jetty while the ship's company snatched a few hours sleep. When the boiler room was opened the following day the bodies of the watch were found in their positions as if they were performing their normal duties. They were reverently removed for burial.'

Captain Gordon, in the throes of getting his ship seaworthy in the shortest possible time, still found time to organise a funeral with full military honours for *Exeter*'s dead that afternoon in the European cemetery at Kembang Koening.

'The whole of the boiler room was covered with fuel oil from deckplates to bulkheads and even on the deckhead. It was impossible to work in there for long periods owing to the fumes from the oil. Eventually two fans were brought into action, these effectively cleared the air and a gang of native labourers cleaned the boiler room. After much feverish activity and improvisation two more boilers were made available at which time, as I had been detailed for watch I left the scene of activity to take a hurried snack.'

Ted notes that all day long while the repairs were going on Japanese reconnaissance planes kept them under constant surveillance, annoying the gunners again by keeping just out of range.

It seemed that the Japanese were unstoppable in their determination to invade Java but the overall ABDAFLOAT commander, Admiral Helfrich decided to regroup his forces and ordered *Perth* and *Houston* to join the ships defending the western end of Java. At the same time *Exeter* was told to make her escape via the Sunda Strait, taking with her the American destroyer *Pope* and the *Encounter*. All five ships sailed on the 28th; *Perth* and *Houston* in the morning and *Exeter* with her consorts after dark.

At 2300 that evening Captain Waller, with *Perth* and *Houston* sighted a number of Japanese transports and charged into them with guns firing. Two ships were sunk and two forced to beach. But by this time the Jap warships were upon them; four cruisers and ten destroyers. Try as they might there was no escape and just after midnight *Perth* was hit by four torpedoes that sent her to the bottom. *Houston,* with her two remaining turrets dead, was hit by three torpedoes and, at 0025, her skipper, Captain Rooks gave the order to abandon ship and she sank about twenty minutes later.

When *Exeter, Pope* and *Encounter* set out, Captain Gordon knew that with the Jap's complete dominance of the sea and air there was little chance of them ever reaching safety. Ted and his shipmates also knew.

'We set sail in brilliant moonlight......[about which] the language was rich in nautical terms and extremely lurid. Shortly after we sailed the captain informed us over the ship's radio extension that we were about to make a "getaway". The news was welcome but the outcome of the venture was doubtful because we knew that the Japs would have ships waiting for us whenever we left port.

'During the first watch work in the boiler room was completed, making two more boilers ready and giving us a speed of twenty-two knots. As we had taken on oil fuel we were at our maximum draught, which meant that we could not sail through the Bali Straits [the nearest exit from the Java Sea] as there was insufficient depth. The alternative course for our dash to freedom lay through the Sunda Straits.

'To the joy of everyone dark clouds began to obscure the moon; violent scattered showers beat down upon us and our hopes began to rise. Lookouts reported shadowy shapes during the night but our luck seemed to be holding out and no contact was made.

'The long hours stretched into Sunday morning and as my watch mates were waiting for their reliefs and I was entering the 8 o'clock readings in the Engine Room Register, the loudspeakers blared; "Two enemy cruisers and destroyers in sight!"

'My relief came down in double quick time to allow me to snatch a cup of tea before the fireworks began. There was no time for the two eggs on offer for breakfast but in any case I was too excited to eat them at the time. However I had only been at action stations for a short while when the loudspeaker announced; "Enemy craft not now in sight."

'The fire party with whom I was stationed breathed a sigh of relief, reflecting my own feelings. But it was only temporary relief because we all sensed that our biggest dread, that of being trapped in the Java Sea, was about to become a reality.

'An hour later, after a preliminary crackling the loudspeaker announced: "Enemy cruisers in sight!"

[This brief announcement did not overstate the case. There were in fact four cruisers and three destroyers, outgunning *Exeter* by forty guns to six.]

In the true tradition of the destroyer's role, both *Pope* and *Encounter* tried to shield the battered cruiser with smoke screens. But the enemy had the advantage, not only in speed and guns, as they were also able to divide and attack the damaged ship from both sides. Nevertheless Captain Gordon was able to dodge the inevitable end for a time; and while the destroyers fended off a torpedo attack *Exeter* even managed to blow the stern off one of the attackers.

Down below the fire party stood by, Ted setting an example to the others.

'Our gunfire soon produced the usual chaos on the stoker's messdeck. Frequently we were shaken by near misses which caused the chains on the ladder to the upper deck to rattle ominously. Suspense mounted among the fire party. It was not difficult to appreciate their mood. We were herded together below unable to witness what was happening overhead and waiting to be hit before we could do anything. Our impotence was most frustrating. To impress the younger members of our gathering I made a pretence of examining the flooding cabinet with a nonchalance I was far from feeling. We were waiting, waiting, waiting for what we knew to be inevitable.'

The end was to come in exactly two hours. With the action commencing at 0935, at 1120 there was an explosion that wrecked the power systems and started uncontrollable fires.

'The suspense continued for two long hours. Near misses seem to lift the old lady clear of the water. It was not difficult to imagine water pouring in through the ship's side at any moment. Suddenly she gave a violent lurch followed by a series of awful vibrations as if she were in mortal agony, as indeed she was. We were hit in "A" boiler room, not very far from where we were stationed and where we had risked using another boiler with badly sagging superheater tubes which had increased our speed to 26 knots at the time we were hit. This wretched luck cast us down. We had been in two actions in two days and been hit in both boiler rooms. It was most discouraging to think that the Japs had had all the good fortune in our actions against them. Man for man we felt equal to our adversaries.

'The situation appeared to be hopeless and what made matters worse there were no fires in our part of ship for us to deal with. We simply had to stay at our stations and wait for orders.'

At 1135 Captain Gordon gave the order to abandon 'the old lady', as Anderson affectionately calls her and his nightmare scenario of drowning his mates became reality.

'The loudspeaker gave its preliminary crackle and the order came: "Sink the ship. Flood all magazines. Abandon ship!"

'The Chief Petty Officer in charge of the magazine crew had often discussed with me the possibility of flooding magazines; and over and over again I promised that should the occasion arise, I would allow the crew to make good their escape before I used the huge wheel spanner to open the great valve in the bottom of the ship. To my overwhelming delight I saw the whole of the magazine crew quite safe a few minutes later.

'I reached the upper deck in quick time; I don't remember my feet touching the steps of the companionway. The thunder of the guns of five enemy cruisers and six destroyers struck me like a blow and the whine of shrapnel was terrifying. I could see the flash from the muzzles of the guns and puffs of brown smoke which followed. Every one of those shells directed towards the ship I thought was heading for me!

'By the time I arrived on the upper deck all the Carley rafts had been released. Men were diving overboard the whole length of the ship and I joined them without hesitation. When I surfaced I noticed my slippers floating by my ears and I let them drift away; an action I was to regret before many days passed.

'The ship appeared to be a long way from me as I suppose she was travelling at fifteen knots when I left her. Dense black smoke was issuing from her funnels, shells raised great gouts of water on either side of her but she steamed on, defying the enemy to the very last.

'Some shells pitched uncomfortably close to me, their detonation causing giant fingers to grasp my chest in a merciless hold, driving out every breath of air from my lungs so that I was left weak and gasping, scarcely able to remain afloat. Fortunately a raft bore down on me and I was able to clamber aboard. At that very moment Bernard Preece our scrum half came in over the other side. We paddled around picking up other survivors and in a short time we had a full load.'

No sailor likes to see any ship sink and if it is his own, with which he has lived in a sort of symbiotic relationship of protector and protected, has come to know her every foible and, as in the case

A cluster of bombs astern.(Anderson)

The last of the 'old lady'. Photo taken from a Japanese aircraft (IWM)

of the engine room staff, has heard her every heart-beat, it is like witnessing the death of a relative. Such was the case with Edward Anderson and the ship's company of *Exeter*.

'Three enemy destroyers hove in sight, their aircraft were active overhead and our eyes were drawn back to the ship. Enemy gunfire was wide of the mark, it was agonising to watch the splash of salvos with no apparent hits. "Dear old lady," I thought "when will they grant you a merciful release?"

'Suddenly the smoke from her funnels changed to lurid tongues of flame. A bomber released his bombs but the old ship sailed on. Then I watched her death throes as a torpedo hit her. She listed gradually [to starboard] as if still reluctant to die. Finally she heeled right over on her side and was lost to sight in a flurry of foam. It was a relief to see her go. She met her end honourably and tenaciously, crippled and helpless as she had been. We were very proud of her.'

Exeter's consorts were to share the same fate. *Encounter*, now having the undivided attention of the cruisers went down with colours flying and guns blazing. The old four funnel American destroyer *Pope* managed to evade the enemy by taking advantage of the cover of a rain squall. But not for long; because as she steered for the Lombok Strait and escape, the ever-present Japanese floatplanes spotted her. Shortly after she was attacked by dive bombers and high level planes and with ammunition exhausted and his ship sinking under him, the skipper Captain Blinn, ordered abandon ship. The inevitable Japanese cruiser then arrived to send her to the bottom with gunfire; the last of Admiral Doorman's force that had set out from Sourabaya a very long day earlier. Perhaps it was just as well that the name ABDA*FLOAT* had been quietly dropped some time before.

CHAPTER 2

The Camp at Macassar

As Ted sat in the Carley raft among his shipmates, watching the Exeter *disappear beneath the sea, inconsequential thoughts came to his head. He wondered what had happened to the two ducks that had 'joined' the ship a few weeks previously. They had become a familiar sight waddling around the quarterdeck. Had they come through the action? Ted hoped they had been able to fly or swim to their own freedom.*

A strong tide was flowing and a fairish breeze was getting up which made it very difficult to keep the head of the raft into the wind. Our raft had been punctured by shrapnel and as it was fully loaded the hole was under water and it began to sink. So Bernard and I swam to another less loaded raft nearby.

There was an anxious moment when spotter planes swooped down and circled low over us. Were they just checking or were they going to use their machine guns on us? Taking no chances I dived into the water and under the raft and stayed down as long as I could. I came up to fill my lungs with air again only to find the aircraft still circling the rafts and the occupants actually waving to us. I wondered if it was out of sympathy or derision.

The planes flew off and Ted got into the raft again but now in mid-afternoon the greatest hazard was from the sun.

We were all stripped to the waist and some of the young stokers and boys were moaning with the agony of sunburn from a tropical sun that blazed from a brilliant blue sky. Bernard suggested that so many men should get into the water and we should take turns in swimming to get our bodies out of the sun. My problem was my bald head and so I kept dipping it in the sea to try and keep it cool. But despite all my efforts the top of my head got badly burnt. For a while I ceased to take an interest in what was going on around me and I lost all count of time. Bernard told me afterwards that I was saying all kinds of ridiculous things.

Once someone began a scare when he thought he saw a shark – the Java Sea is noted for them. This caused a panic among those in the water as they all frantically tried to get back into the raft. Then someone suggested that the underwater explosions of so many shells would keep them away, a bit of common sense that calmed everyone down.'

Another scare for those in the water was the passing close by of a sea snake.'—a yellow and black banded creature, this caused another frantic exodus from the sea.' *But things gradually settled down and they went back to their anti-sunburn routine until rescue came.*

A Japanese destroyer hove in sight and came alongside us; her decks thronged with our survivors. We climbed on board by the scrambling nets which were suspended over the side of the destroyer. As each man arrived on board he was stripped of watches and rings.

I had never been face to face with a Japanese and I was interested to see one at close quarters. As I looked at the curious ape-like men who strutted about with all the arrogance of little fighting cocks Mr Churchill's words came to mind: 'funny little brown men.' But these little men were not at all funny as they used their rifle butts against their well nigh naked and helpless prisoners.

When all the survivors in the vicinity had been taken aboard, the destroyer proceeded on her way. We were given some biscuits and water and as dusk descended we were herded forward to a corticene laid deck, which was to be our temporary quarters. That night I slept soundly on the bare deck and woke as dawn was breaking. It was such a glorious spectacle that I temporarily forgot the circumstances in which I found myself. Later tea without milk or sugar was served from large tins and biscuits were again handed round but only the selfish few got any and I could see the law of the jungle coming into effect and it looked like the survival of the fittest.

Later in the forenoon we came to a lush green island where there was an oil tanker to which the destroyer secured and immediately started taking on fuel. The whole of our party was then transferred to the oiler where we spent the rest of the forenoon trying to escape the burning rays of the sun. The effects of our exposure on the raft were apparent on all sides. Some of us were as red as newly boiled lobsters and several fainted in the heat.

Some time later the tanker crew rigged an awning over the deck which provided some shade and alleviated much of our suffering. But then thirst began to torment us until three large metal containers were placed on the deck. Once again the law of the jungle prevailed as the men squabbled and fought over the single mug that was provided. The appearance of a few more tins, either provided by the Japs or scrounged by our more enterprising members, eased the situation.

Later in the evening a Dutch hospital ship the *Optenoorte* (sic) arrived and dropped anchor. We were immediately transferred to her in invasion barges and herded on to her deck. That night I slept on the forecastle with my particular chum the Bandmaster [Bandmaster Vidler] in the company of rats and cockroaches. Next morning we managed to wash ourselves under a salt water tap. It felt sticky and we did not feel clean or refreshed afterwards. But at least we felt cool for a while.

By noon we were ravenous and food became the only thought and was the sole subject of conversation. A handful of sticky rice was given to each man and groups of ten had to share a small tin of meat.

Ted could not stomach the rice but his small portion of meat revived him 'greatly'. Curiously, he was unable to eat the rice for some time in spite of a starvation diet of very little else.

I grew to dread mealtimes. Every time I smelled the rice I felt sick and every vestige of appetite left me. But later in the week a portion of real bread and some sweet black coffee was given to each of us. This was a marvellous day for me as was also the occasion when we were given rice flavoured with apricots. These were the only times when I actually ate all my portion of food to the disappointment of an eager band of followers who, aware of my distaste for the fare, hung around for my leavings.

Water was a great problem as it was necessary to wait in a long queue in the bowels of the ship. The heat was overpowering and it was a common occurrence to see people faint in the queue. To fill a bottle one had to climb a flight of stairs at the head of which stood a large pot of water guarded by armed sailors, some of whom knew a few words of English that they were keen to practise upon us. When Bandy and I went to fill our bottles, a sentry said to us, 'Come here!'

'Act green,' I whispered out of the corner of my mouth.

To act green in the navy is to play the innocent.

We pretended not to understand and tried to look as vacant as cod fish and they gave up.

As we lay at anchor off Banjermassen, as the place was called, the shore seemed invitingly close but a glance over the side dispelled any thoughts of escape for huge sharks maintained a constant patrol around the ship. Then after a week we weighed anchor and a day and a half later arrived at Macassar in the Celebes, where the ship made fast and we were disembarked and assembled on the jetty to be mustered.

The sun blazed down from a cloudless sky roasting the flagstones of the jetty. I found it impossible to stand still as the stones were too hot for my bare feet. Bandy, who had not kicked off his plimsolls when abandoning ship, let me stand on his feet until we were ordered to move off.

The captain led the way with his officers and his tatterdemalion crew followed. As is usual when a long line of people is on the march gaps appeared in the ragged files and it was often necessary for the stragglers to run to catch up with the main body. Those who dropped to the rear were viciously beaten with clubs or the butts of rifles wielded by the shambling Japanese soldiers.

To add to the nightmarish quality of the march the sun had melted the tarmac in patches not shaded by overhanging trees. We were not allowed to avoid these patches and those with bare feet were burnt by the melted tar. When some tried to stop and bind their feet with the long grass growing on the side of the road, the clubs and rifle butts were brought into action.

This was the first instance of brutality by one man on another that I had ever seen and at first I could not believe the evidence of my eyes. However, as I was to witness it again and again and have personal experience I came to know it was not a dream but stark reality. The march went on for about three or four miles to the barracks of the local Indonesian garrison, the whole route being lined with jeering, taunting natives waving the Japanese flag whilst Jap officials recorded the scene with cine cameras.

On arrival at the camp we were quartered in buildings which were divided into cubicles about ten foot long by seven foot wide, a central gangway giving access to them. Six men were allocated to each cubicle and Bandy and I shared ours with two seamen, and two Air Arm men. Conditions were spartan to say the least. The floor was of stone and bare of furniture and the walls whitewashed. But it was good to be able to flop down on the cool stone deck and ease our blistered feet.

For our first meal we were given some biscuits and fortunately there was an abundant supply of good sweet water. Bandy helped me to the make-shift bathroom where we both had a good swill down. There was no need for towels, even if we had one, for we dried off almost immediately. That night we slept on the stone floor and despite the discomfort I slept well.

Next morning, to my joy, we were given half a breakfast roll and though small it was something that I could eat. As we ate we discussed what the future had in store for us and it seemed certain that the Japs would find some sort of work for us. But at the moment it seemed they had no immediate plans. The question also arose regarding the possibility of our being moved to other camps and an air of uncertainty hung over us all.

Although my feet were terribly burnt and sore from the march, I was anxious to see what our prison looked like. Bandy helped me to walk a short distance so that I could have a look around. The camp was surrounded by tall trees and within the perimeter there were green lawns interspersed with trees. There were numerous coconut palms and banana trees in the camp all bearing fruit which we could only admire, being denied to us by sentries with rifle and bayonet. Near the lavatories grew patches of jasmine whose fragrance scented the night air; and when the breeze was favourable it was wafted through our hut. In other circumstances it would have been a delightful setting for a camp. There was an abundant supply of good fresh water, showers were available and most important of all there was good sanitation. This last greatly uplifted me because one of my greatest dreads was to be cooped up in close contact with others with no sanitary facilities available.

That evening we were given some repulsive smoky rice and a fragment of stinking fish which left me feeling sick. But in the morning we were given a whole roll each which revived my spirits and we wolfed them down in case the Japs found they had made a mistake and took them back.

Ted and the others gradually settled into a routine but for some while Ted could not come to terms with the food.

To supplement our evening meals some green leaves were introduced that looked like boiled lily leaves. We ate twice a day, the first meal consisting of a small bread roll whilst the second was made up of rice and sometimes half a banana or a piece of cucumber. It was brought to the hut in two large tins which were difficult to carry because the rice was so hot. Several times the tins were dropped and much of the ration was wasted until Bill Eddy our Chief Electrician and Roy Ruse the Chief EA contrived an ingenious carrying device from a length of wire and there was no more spillage after that.

I couldn't face the rice so I used to keep half my breakfast roll for the evening. For a month or so I survived on a bread roll and two or three bottles of water a day. At first I was worried about constipation; but a word from one of our ship's doctors put it into perspective, 'If you don't put fuel on a fire you don't have any ashes.'

We ate our food from pieces of paper or cloth until some of the unoccupied buildings were raided for plates, cups or spoons and the purloined gear pooled so that all in our hut had the use of a plate as well as a fork or spoon at mealtimes. One of our chaps found a small enamel chamberpot in which he collected his food which was at first a subject of much comment until the others got used to the sight.

There was nearly always a little food left over after it had been doled out and it was perhaps inevitable but nevertheless unedifying to see grown men squabbling over small portions of extra food. But after a while any little item which was too small or could not be shared equally was cut for with playing cards or by drawing lots.

By now the Japs had overcome their initial curiosity about us and began to assert their authority. Cases of beating of unprecedented ferocity became increasingly common. There was no apparent reason for this behaviour. It was generally considered by us that, Japs being physically smaller on the whole, they were trying to boost their egos by this treatment of their bigger captives. Our Navigating Officer took upon himself the task of trying to improve conditions for us and was responsible for stopping much of the brutality of the guards. Often when he saw one of our men being beaten he would step in and take the place of the victim. The Japs had a most incomprehensible mentality; it didn't matter who they were beating as long as it was somebody. Every day they indulged in various forms of physical abuse, one favourite form of which was to make our fellows do press ups and as they got weaker and failed to lift themselves, they were hit across the base of the spine with a cane or shortened billiard cue. Another entertainment was stabbing lighted cigarette ends into the bare backs of their victims. Nor was their cruelty confined to human beings; an unfortunate monkey in a cage was outrageously savaged by them and left cowed and motionless on the bottom of its cage. Yet sometimes the Japs revealed astounding flashes of kindness by giving prisoners cigarettes or buying them eggs; but this was not a regular feature of their conduct. They derived more pleasure by torturing us than contributing to our welfare.

After being in the camp for about two weeks each man was given a small tablet of soap and each cubicle two toothbrushes and two towels. We decided to draw lots for the toothbrushes and my usual bad luck in games prevailed. I had to continue rubbing my teeth daily with a piece of cloth.

By this time beards and moustaches had sprouted luxuriantly but although my beard was quite respectable, my moustache was stiff and curled into my mouth. It was ginger in colour and simply would not be trained. In comparison, the fellows who had looted razors looked immaculately clean. Others who had found knives spent hours whetting them on stones to a razor edge in order to shave themselves and their friends; so I enlisted the aid of one these chaps to rid me of my moustache and beard.

To combat boredom some people made games like draughts, chess and Ludo [*called Uckers in the navy, it had far more complicated rules than the civilian version*]. Others spent weeks polishing pretty stones which were to be found in the roadway. There was a craze for making sundials and they could be seen everywhere. We had three outside our hut; one of them surprisingly accurate, indicating the hours by means of coloured glass fragments. Another was a workmanlike construction of wood suspended on the wall. But the piece de resistance was an elaborate masterpiece set out on the ground, the hours and quarters marked by small pebbles and the whole surrounded with complicated ornamentation.

Aware of Bandy's passion for music and my own interest in the subject, I often encouraged him to speak about it and he would hold forth on the subject for hours on end and as I am a good listener we made an ideal pair.

Had the camp been situated in less congenial surroundings our lot would have been far less bearable. But the setting of the camp did in some way offset the continual gnawing hunger and the behaviour of the guards.

Ted and the others were very much incensed by the privileges that the Dutch prisoners appeared to have over the others. One extraordinary aspect was that the Dutch officers were allowed to retain their swords in captivity, which they wore around the camp. Ted was also amazed at the large numbers of Dutch and Indonesians who wore Red Cross arm bands.

I estimated that there were about 2,000 men in the camp comprising British, American, Indonesians and Dutch. These last were the well-to-do of the community; they had everything a prisoner could desire. It was rumoured that some of them had been allowed to walk off their ships with all their belongings and it was also said that a Dutch destroyer had actually surrendered to a Jap minesweeper. Whether true or not, neither rumour improved our opinion of them. What made matters worse was the fact that the Dutchmen seemed to have access to provisions of all kinds which they openly carried to their huts without any reaction from the Japs. The Dutch political internees and navy personnel in particular regarded us with a thinly veiled hostility and never showed any concern for any of our sick men. They waxed and grew fat while we became thinner. As time went on some added insult to injury by asking, 'Why are the English so thin?'.

They had an irritating aloofness which was annoying in the extreme. Ron, my cubicle mate referred to them as 'Germans with their brains kicked out'. These smug well-fed Dutchmen looked at us as if we were social outcasts and any onlooker would have thought that they were the captors and we the prisoners. I think they were aware of their obesity because every morning they attempted physical exercises. But with their flabby paunches shuddering at the slightest exertion, after a few minutes they were reduced to masses of perspiring blubber. Anglo-Dutch relations were far from cordial and remained so all the time we were with them.

The natives that lived around the camp were willing to sell food to the prisoners through the wire, a dangerous practice for buyer and seller as both were severely punished if they were caught and of course money and goods were confiscated; but despite the risk trade still continued. The Americans proved to be good business men. They bought goods at the fence and sold them on to those who were too timid to conduct their own business. If you had money there were all sorts of goods to be bought; doughnuts, coffee, sugar, milk, potatoes, banana fritters and tobacco. The Indonesian prisoners did well with this trading; in fact probably better than the Americans as they were dealing with their own people. They were also inveterate gamblers and at night their quarters resembled a casino where hectic gambling enriched the fortunate and impoverished the rest.

Our cubicle was particularly poor. All I possessed was a blue shirt and a pair of overall trousers, for which I had traded some of my rice ration. Bandy had a few odd coppers and a fifty cent Ceylon piece which was worthless in this part of the world. Barny,

Taff, Smithy and Ron could raise a grand total of four guilders (worth about 50p at that time) and being inveterate smokers spent it all on tobacco. Other cubicles managed to get tea from some mysterious source which they boiled and reboiled and finally when it had lost all flavour they smoked it. As time went on smokers found it increasingly difficult to get paper for their cigarettes and we had to guard our few books and other reading material closely, otherwise they went up in smoke as well.

Before they had evacuated the town the Dutch had destroyed anything of use or value and the Japs now demanded working parties to clear the resulting debris, open up the roads and coal and store ships in the harbour. The work was hard and the guards enjoyed showing off to the public by clubbing the prisoners with their rifle butts whenever they could. During unguarded moments however, those with money were able to buy all sorts of things from sympathetic onlookers.

One of the things that POWs in the Far East missed was reliable news from the outside world. Failing that, any 'news' was better than none at all for the purposes of morale. So while in Pudu Gaol, Malaya, Padre Noel Duckworth relayed glad tidings to the prisoners from a fictitious 'well-dressed Eurasian'(Naked Island, Russell Braddon, Werner-Laurie 1952) Ted and his companions relied on the working parties to satisfy what he calls, 'a second hunger—an insatiable desire for news.' Daily he noted in his diary the current rumours, mostly preposterous; as well as the trading that went on.

'<u>Monday 30th March.</u> Wonderful morning and very pleasant walking in the shade of the trees. First on list for late meal today: rice, one boiled potato, portion of fried beef about the size of a thumbnail, a spoonful of green weedy stuff (identity unknown) a piece of marrow the size of an Oxo cube, or a sweet potato. I drew the marrow. Dysentery has broken out and yesterday one of the signalmen died of it. Scabies and crabs are also prevalent. Thank goodness we have plenty of running water and some soap; my greatest dread is to become lousy. Today's rumours:

1. Turkey is at war with the Axis powers and has launched an offensive against Bulgaria.

2. Tokyo and Yokohama have been bombed from Vladivostok and Formosa.

3. New Guinea has been heavily bombed.

'It's also rumoured that the captain, commander and heads of departments are to be taken to Japan for interrogation, also some telegraphist ratings.'

This last did come true and was a severe blow to us; the captain and heads of departments, including Navvy our champion [the Navigating Officer, Lieutenant Commander Hudson] were to be sent to Japan. It was thanks to Navvy's courage and insistence that we were able to walk around the camp from dawn to dusk without interference from the guards, unless of course some offence had been committed by one of our number. I shall never forget how miserable we all felt when the skipper visited us to say goodbye.

On the evening of the same day we were registered by the Japs, giving them details of nationality, name and age, ship, where rescued, birth place, wounds and money and valuables. We gave this information to a little man dressed in shorts which came below his knees. He repeated everything we said and then put it down on paper using a brush and, something which fascinated us, writing in queer hieroglyphics from right to left. We felt in a better frame of mind after this because it seemed that news of of our safety might be sent home and thus relieve our loved ones of their anxiety.

At first our chief worry had been constipation due to the lack of food but after a while dysentery broke out. The sufferers were sent to a room which we fondly called the sick bay which had been opened earlier but soon ran out of supplies. The first victim was one of our signalmen, a fine young man who died in agony, misery and filth. Scabies then made its unwelcome appearance and then to add to our discomfiture, body vermin. I was glad there was plenty of water and some soap because one of my dreads (apart from being mutilated or permanently incapacitated) was to be lousy. Daily I searched my clothes for unwelcome visitors and for a while at least I remained clean.

As Bandy and Taff had some knowledge of first aid they were called to help in the sick bay. This proved to be most helpful because toasting and brewing tea or coffee made great inroads into our existing stocks of firewood. Bandy and Taff now had access to unlimited supplies. I used to wait until dusk and scramble through the wire to the sickbay, collect the wood and smuggle it back to our hut.

Bandy became a patient among those he was trying to help and was the first in our hut to go down with dysentery. When I visited him in the isolation room he had a ghastly appearance which frightened me. Fortunately he made a good recovery and was soon able to continue with ministering to the other patients. His natural flair for organisation made him invaluable to the doctors and also, being an excellent bridge player he was always in demand at night when the doctors played.

'Wednesday 1st April. Very pleasant early in the morning but hot later in the afternoon. One of Navvy's ideas before he left was to start a daily lecture in each block, to be given by people who had unusual occupations in civvy street, interesting hobbies or anything that would relieve the demoralising boredom of our lives. I listened to my first one today (the system has been under way for about a week). This was given by one of the lads and was on diving and was both interesting and entertaining. A talk on the experiences of a hotel porter completely took us out of ourselves.

'Later Bandy did some watch repairing at which he is quite an expert. [In the afternoon] Had our bath just in time to see a most unpalatable dirty, burnt and smoky rice being served out. My portion of fish consisted of a head complete with eyes and covered all over with egg like deposits. The rice was impermeated with a smell of rotting fish. Even for prison camp fare this was absolutely vile. Was mighty glad I had saved half my breakfast roll.

'Watched a game of basket ball between the Javanese and Dutch. Shortly after there was an issue of a small piece of sour bread per man, this apparently being the promised third meal demanded on our behalf by Navvy before he left. It was reported that the Dutch had been issued with rice, bread, eggs and coffee. There followed an altercation at the galley from which however came no satisfaction. Later it was confessed that a mistake had been made. To balance our disappointment Bandy and I received an unexpected invitation from the Taffs' cubicle. Young Taff had been on duty in the galley that morning and had won sundry beans, yams and rice. These were boiled and I must confess I downed my beans and yams with great relish—the rice as yet fails to attract me.'

When the working parties returned in the evenings they were besieged by the others for rumours they might have heard in the town. Some were passed to them by friendly inhabitants when the guards were not looking but other prisoners were supposed to have heard the news on the wireless. However no one was able to give a definite source for his information.

One day Tommy, one of the fellows in our cubicle, returned to the hut fuming after he had been working in the town under a Jap civilian who could speak English.

'I suppose you are all homesick but never mind, you will soon be home. We have taken Hawaii and the American fleet has been destroyed. England and America are on the verge of capitulation.'

He continued in this vein all the time the party was working although even the most credulous could not believe him. As if in opposition there appeared a native carrying a small placard on which was written: 'Be brave. Your friends are near. Keep your chins up. Your friends are coming.' This he showed the boys whenever the guards had their backs turned.

In those early days of the war [1942] we heard that Russia had invaded Rumania, the Americans had landed in the Celebes, Russia had declared war on the Japanese, Russia had penetrated far into Germany, Turkey had declared war on Germany, seven English divisions had landed in France. None of this was true of course but we all brightened considerably when these rumours went the rounds. We felt that within the week or so the allies would be at our gates.

But food for the body rather than the mind was the greatest priority. Hunger gradually changed to starvation as each person's reserves of fat were used up. The talk and thoughts of everyone were about food. Ted, with his hatred of the rice and his seeming inability to stomach it was getting very near the point of collapse.

Continual hunger began to shatter my 'super-optimism' and one by one the thoughts that I had entertained for the future dissolved into nothingness. The long hours of waiting from seven in the morning to five at night for even a little wholesome food, only to be greeted by the sight and smell of detestable rice deprived me of any appetite I may have had. Sometimes I was able to swap the rice for a portion of fruit which had been included in our rations; but I could feel the effects of starvation quite clearly. I was becoming deaf, there was a deterioration in my mental reflexes and my heart palpitated at the least exertion. When I stood up quickly I blacked out, or when I looked up at the sky the clouds receded at an alarming rate and my head started to spin so that I had to sit down. I felt old and useless in sharp contrast to only a few weeks before when I had been playing rugger.

'Thursday 2nd April. Red letter day today. Breakfast consisted of one and a half sardines in tomato sauce and a fairly large hunk of bread. Most wonderful and succulent meal since Easter. ......Had recourse to the epsoms before turning in.'

'<u>Friday 3rd.</u> Another feast this morning, more sardines and bread. Highly satisfactory results from the epsoms........Another fresh crowd of Dutch prisoners arrived. They were immediately besieged to change notes, 10 cent pieces are scarcer than 5 and 10 guilder notes. The rest of our shipmates arrived today. It was good to see so many familiar faces. Discovered that 62 of our crew were lost altogether but considering the severity of the action this seems quite miraculous. Sam is at present in the hospital ship with dysentery. 2nd meal consisted of rice, two boiled potatoes and an Oxo cube sized piece of beef. Made a satisfactory meal with a piece of bread saved from breakfast. Rained steadily until the late meal which was more rice and a tiny piece of native sugar the size of a thumbnail for six men. we cut cards for it and Barney won.'

But odd reminders of the past revived his interest in life after prison.

The long slanting rays of the late afternoon sun reminded me of camping days of old and made me determined that I would live to experience them again, in spite of what these little men could do to me. I resolved that I would always try to be cheerful. I would beat the futility of prison life, useless and boring though it was. I also decided that I would have to eat in order to live. My friends had started commenting upon my ghastly appearance. So I fought my repugnance and ate all the vile fare [*presumably the rice*] but nature gave me a sharp warning that all was not well and at the next meal I ate less and was able to retain it.

One evening I received an invitation from an American friend.

'Come on over. We've got some special chow tonight.'

When I entered his hut there was a delicious aroma of cooking. A steaming pile of meat and sweet potatoes was placed before me and I was told to eat it and ask no questions. When the meal was over my friend asked me what I thought of their cooking.

'Delicious. But where did you get the meat?' I asked.

'I guess you've just eaten the camp commandant's dog!'

For a moment I felt vaguely uneasy but gradually a feeling of well-being came over me and the cares of the world were forgotten as I realised that I was no longer hungry. The next day I suffered for my gluttony as my stomach, having contracted with so little use made a vigorous protest.

With his eyes now opened, Ted saw there was a singular absence of dogs and cats around the camp. He was saddened by the effects hunger had on some of his fellow prisoners, making them 'revert to the primitive'.

I saw a parcel smuggled into a hut and in the bustle a doughnut fell out on to the ground. In a flash one of the men seized it and tore at it with his teeth, his flashing eyes holding us at bay, daring us to deprive him of his prize. In peace time this man was an accountant. There was always a flock of scavengers in the vicinity of the galley; fights broke out over the meagre contents of the waste bins.

The men in the cubicle opposite ours volunteered to become servants of the Japs. One undertook the task of repairing their bicycles, two more acted as mess boys while the other four kept the Japs's hut clean and fanned them at mealtimes. They were generously rewarded for their industry and often returned to their cubicle with tins of fruit and salmon as well as tea and coffee; all of which they kept to themselves. When Japs visited them in their cubicles the ensuing servility was sickening to watch; as was the sight of others who followed the Japs waiting for them to drop the butts of their cigarettes; or others who saluted these irritating little monkeys for a whole cigarette.

Navy habits were therapeutic in settling their daily lives into something bearable.

To relieve the boredom, we worked to a fixed routine. Each day a duty cubicle in the hut was responsible for bringing the food from the galley and distributing it fairly among the cubicles. The food containers had to be cleaned and returned to the galley, dishes had to be washed and the hut and its surrounding area cleaned up generally.

Bandy and I also developed a daily routine; up by just after seven o'clock, down mosquito net and wash without soap. (the small tablet we were allowed was for a month but it lasted only a few days.) Clean our teeth with a piece of rag. After breakfast, wash clothes which dried immediately in the brilliant sunshine. Then a stroll in the shade of the palm trees and general relaxation for a couple of hours. At 3.30 a shower; then we dawdled until the evening meal after which we joined two of our Welsh chums, Taff Davis and Tommy Thomas to swap and discuss rumours and put world affairs in their proper perspective. In the early days we spent the evenings sitting in the moonlight until talk of home and overwhelming nostalgia, or hordes of ravenous mosquitoes, drove us in to our cubicles. Then, with our mosquito net affording us the ultimate sanctuary we succumbed to the oblivion of slumber.

Bandy was able to keep himself in tobacco by repairing watches, which kept him occupied while I obtained another book called 'Bosambo of the River'. As well as reading it slowly to savour every word I copied huge chunks in copperplate writing.

Another interest for Ted was a young Dutchman with whom he became friendly.

My young Dutch friend was called Edgar. He was very different in outlook from his fellow countrymen in that he was kind and sympathetic. He came to our cubicle originally in search of news. From him I learnt the story of the capitulation of the Dutch army in the Celebes. When danger first threatened the women and children were evacuated to a district that was considered to be out of the danger area. But that part of the country was quickly overrun by the Japs who then demanded the surrender of the army otherwise the women and children would be massacred. Colonel Jan Orloog the Dutch commander agreed providing that he was given an honourable surrender, meaning that the troops should be permitted to retain their arms. This was granted but the troops had their arms taken from them when they reached Macassar, although the officers kept their swords.

Edgar was eager to learn all about Devon and Cornwall and as this was my particular country I was able to help him. He was very well educated and could speak four languages fluently. He started to teach me Dutch and I looked forward to his visits as the mental stimulus was most beneficial and helped me to forget my worries. It was pleasant to entertain a stranger amid the bustle of the cleaning up operations with the chaps whistling and singing as they worked.

One of the pastimes allowed us and enjoyed by all was the boxing which took place under the palm trees, in a natural ring with a tree in each corner and the green velvety turf underfoot. There was never any lack of volunteers and how I envied the participants their energy. Nip officers often watched the contestants trying to knock each other's blocks off.

Another source of enjoyment was to watch the basket ball played on one of the beautiful little patches of lawn which we named Coconut Grove. I was amazed to see such an exhibition of energy. Once when I felt fit I played in an English versus Americans game. We lost 6-0. We didn't know the rules and horrified spectators and our opponents alike when we introduced a bright five minutes of rugger tactics. The referee blew his whistle until he turned purple but nobody took any notice of him while the Yanks enjoyed the skylark tremendously. After the game I was exhausted, my heart was performing in an alarming manner so I decided I wouldn't repeat such an act of folly.

As the men's physical condition got worse due to starvation it was inevitable that disease should spread even though as had been said, there was plenty of water and the sanitation was good.

Whether it was owing to the climate or the poor condition of our blood, each little scratch festered into a weeping sore at an alarming rate. My right foot became swollen enormously through an infected mosquito bite. In addition I was deaf for a few weeks. There was little or no treatment nor were there any dressings or bandages. Then I succumbed to dysentery.

At first I thought that the basket ball game had overtaxed me until the unmistakable symptoms revealed the real trouble. The excruciating agony, the lost control of any bodily functions, the fear of being far from a WC; the lack of desire to eat or live and above all the distasteful results of such a foul disease. It had become the routine to send the very sick men to the *Optenoorte* but I did not want to leave my environment and for nearly two weeks I endured this living death without reporting sick. Then through Bandy's smuggling me some bismuth tablets from the sick bay I began to improve.

Our doctors, Syred, Wyatt and Ryall were inundated with work but our senior medical officer rarely helped them. It seemed that rank carried weight, even in a prison camp. Our chaplain used to comfort us once a week in church but we rarely saw him otherwise when he could have done much good visiting the sick and consoling the desolate.

The Dutch doctors greatly outnumbered our own and the Dutch always enjoyed priority when treatment was available while our people had to wait as long as two hours out in the sun. At eleven o'clock when all the Dutch had been treated, the medicine and bandages were locked away and we British had to make the best of what remained. Among those attendng the sick bay one could see the effects of prison life on our chaps; sunken eyes, gaunt frames and animal-like expressions. Like the others I had lost a tremendous amount of weight and my hip bones protruded so sharply that it was necessary to use my lifebelt as a pad at night, otherwise sleep would have been impossible. Our lifebelts proved to be a boon for, apart from saving our lives when we were in the water, in prison they served as cushions and pillows. Owing to the complete absence of natural padding, even sitting down was painful without some cushioning.

Life at this time had its normal ups and downs but in his weakened state they were seemed greatly magnified.

During my convalescence I remained very weak and one night when I went across the road to fill a water bottle I stepped into a drain which was invisible in the poor light. It must have been a foot deep and I fell heavily. I returned to the tap to wash and refill the bottle and did the very same thing again. I sat down in the road feeling as weak as a kitten and as helpless as a baby. Then from out of the dark came a cackle of native laughter and I could have cried with sheer frustration.

On a particularly miserable wet, cold evening [when still recovering] I was cooking some toast. The wind kept changing direction and seemed to chase me around no matter where I stood. By the time the toast was ready I was streaming from my nose and my eyes were sore and reddened from the smoke. I felt as if I hadn't a friend in the world. But then my fortunes changed. That evening half a duck egg per man was included in the rations and it happened that there was half an egg to spare, so we decided to cut the cards for it. I drew the king of spades and watched with bated breath as the others drew theirs. But no one else was higher and together with my toast, a whole duck egg made the best meal I had had since leaving the ship. Then Jeff had the better of a deal with a Dutchman and was able to buy 77 grammes of coffee for ten cents. To celebrate, a brew was made and although there was no milk or sugar, to me it was nectar. My fortunes rose to their heights that same evening when Bandy brought me a wicker chair and two books, one by Sax Rohmer and the other by Max Brand. I was immediately in the realms of luxury—a real chair and books.

Trading with the locals still went on both at the fence and in the town by the working parties.

Try as they might the Japs could never suppress trading at the fence. Once nineteen Englishmen were caught and we wondered how the Japs would mete out justice. Surprisingly they agreed to allow our people to punish them as they saw fit. Our officers selected a number of chief and petty officers for this distasteful task. Punishment was by a rope's end as thick as a man's wrist. After this all boxing, basket ball and church services were stopped.

Negotiations to start a canteen were also suspended. It was further announced that if trading continued meals would be stopped. We who had nothing to lose thought that if the Japs had collected money from the prisoners at the very outset these complications would never have arisen. After this trade at the fence suffered a severe recession for a few weeks.

But neither punishment by the Japs nor that (amazingly) meted out by the officers on their own starving men could stop them trying to obtain food. Ted later writes:

Surreptitious trading at the fence soon reached its original level again and would-be purchasers became careless and inevitably this led to discovery. An Indonesian who was caught by a guard was found to have thirty eggs in his possession. These were smashed in the roadway and the unfortunate lad was ordered to kneel down and put his face in the mess. Each time he bent over he was given a cut with a cane on the rump. Another Indonesian who refused to obey an order had his hands tied behind his back and was then tied to a tree in such a fashion that he was standing on tip-toe. He was then beaten with a club by relays of guards after which he was left standing, still on tip-toe for half an hour before he was cut down.

Most offences committed by the prisoners were crimes in the eye of the individual Jap beholder although some official edicts were issued.

Frequently the Japs were particularly vicious in their behaviour towards us.

On one occasion the Yanks found a set of drums and were having a noisy session when a guard pounced on them. By signs he indicated that he wanted the drums to be taken to the guard house and the drummers to wait for him there. The Americans took the drums along and then returned to their quarters. When the Jap arrived at the guard house he was furious to find that the Americans were not there and with some of his colleagues he seized an officer and beat him until he eventually collapsed. They were about to revive him with a bucket of water so that they could continue, when a fellow American step between them and took the punishment. A crowd nearby who were watching a basket ball game saw this and cheered the American. This so enraged the guards that they charged the crowd with rifle and bayonet and finally dispersed them by throwing stones and burst the ball with a bayonet.

Not long after this the Japs surprised one of our men trading with the natives at the perimeter. They stamped his purchases into the ground and beat him until he was ready to drop. Then they threw him all over the road with judo throws and while he lay senseless on the road they kicked him. A Jap has no compunction about kicking a man on the ground; the head, the face, the stomach or the back makes not the slightest difference to him.

One evening a Jap caught one of our boys warming his rice over a fire. Without provocation the Jap kicked over the fire and then started beating the boy with a truncheon. When the boy tried to get away he was pinned to the ground by the truncheon pressed against his throat, nearly suffocating him. He was then thrown to the ground with judo throws after which, held by cooperating Indonesians he was severely flogged. Then followed more judo practice during which his head was repeatedly dashed against the stony road, where finally he was left lying unconscious. We brought him into our cubicle where I spent the night bathing his forehead and fanning him with a plate. Later the next day we were told that two hundred eggs had been stolen from the galley. The Japs had no idea who the culprit was but someone had to be the scapegoat, hence the violent treatment of this boy. No matter how big or small the offence, as long as someone was flogged Nippon justice was satisfied.

'The bastards have had some more bad news.' we would think. 'If they are like this now, what are they going to be like when they are on their knees?' We knew there would be bad times ahead when they were losing the war. It wasn't pleasant to contemplate.

One of the first notice the Japs put up for us to read was as follows:

Announcement

We wish to make known to all prisoners of war the following:
1. If you meet a Japanese officer and you do recognise him, you ought to stand to attention and salute him.
2. If a Japanese officer addresses you, you ought to answer him
    a) in English: Yes Sir.
    b) in Dutch: Ja Mynheer.
    c) in Malay: Ja Toen.

3.   He who does not follow the rules mentioned
above shall be punished with heavy
mortification.

(signed) Mori
Headquarters Japanese Army
Makassar, May 28th 1942.

Heavy mortification was not specified but thereafter their favourite implement of punishment, the baseball bat, came to be known as 'Old Mortification'.

Guards were not only fond of beating the prisoners up for very little reason but their sadism took other forms and sometimes a guard would assert his authority on some trivial pretext.

One of my cubicle mates, Taff Davis dropped a bottle which smashed just outside our hut. A passing guard demonstrated his displeasure by making him pluck by hand all the rank grass which grew around the hut. When he had finished his hands were torn and bleeding.

The Japs goaded us on every conceivable occasion with such pin-pricks. They made us pick up tiny pieces of grass or else small stones from the roadway. Sometimes they would address us in Japanese and because we could not understand them we were slapped across the face.

'Never mind,' I would tell the lads, 'the bastards are losing the war and taking it out on us.'

To make our quarters more comfortable we found some boards to put on the floor of our cubicle. Though hard, they were better to lie on than the cold stone floor. They also raised us above the floor so that we kept dry when heavy rain ran into the huts. We scrubbed the boards every weekend with a brick and water until they were spotless. It was evident that the Japs did not like us enjoying a little comfort and one day a guard motioned for us to take them outside. It was a particularly unpleasant time of year, probably in the monsoon and we did not relish the idea of sleeping on the floor again. So I whispered to Barney (a cubicle mate), 'Act green!'

We raised one of the boards and turned it over as if we were inspecting the other side of it and then replaced it. The guard gave a terrifying grunt and whacked Barney across the stern with his rifle butt. The boards went out in double quick time!

After a few days during which the boards got thoroughly saturated we were allowed to bring them inside again.

Some people were becoming resentful of this senseless

unpredictable behaviour and beginning to hit back in self-defence. The first example of this occurred when three of our men were caught trading by an Indonesian sentry. Two of them escaped, the third striking the guard before he too made off. The authorities ruled that if the offenders did not come forward before a certain time meals would be stopped and we would be locked in our huts from dawn to dusk each day. The delinquents confessed and were dealt with by our own people.

Some of the Indonesians were by now cooperating with the Japs and being used as guards; but instead of carrying rifles and bayonets they were armed with swords. The Japs also decided to use the Indonesian buglers. They sounded reveille at 0700 but this was generally ignored at first until the Japs decided on a daily muster at 0745 before which they went through the huts beating up those they caught in bed. Another bugle call reminded the duty cubicles to clean up the camp and ensure that the drains weren't choked up. Later in the evening another call sent those on duty to the galley for the evening meal and finally at 2300 a long pathetic solo signifying Lights Out was blown. This usually woke us up as we were well away by then and the dusky bugler, together with his bugle, became the subject of a number of suggestions.

Despite the continual beatings and other punishments, as well as the starvation diet, in Ted's judgment 'the camp commandant seemed to be a fairly rational man as far as Japs were concerned'. *This was soon to change with the arrival of Yoshida, an apparently junior addition to the Japanese guards.*

The arrival of 'Gold Tooth' heralded the beginning of a miserable period of our existence. He was a short, ape-like man with ugly features the most prominent of which were teeth encased in gold. He wore a slouch hat and shorts that came well down below his knees, almost to meet the suspenders on his sturdy legs. Of all the Nips we had yet met he was by far the most evil. Feared and hated by all he strutted about like a game cock; his every movement watched and whispered around the camp. He was merciless and beat officers and men alike. One of his first acts was to pluck the moustaches from the faces of two Englishmen with pliers, an atrocity that shocked the whole camp. Not a day passed when Goldy failed to enhance his reputation. One day he saw one of our boys trying the door of the tool shed as he wanted to borrow a saw. Goldy saw him shaking the door as one invariably does when trying a locked door, and thought he was trying to break in. The poor lad was hauled to the guard house and was clubbed thirty times with a baseball bat. Two of his friends who stopped to help him to the sick bay were also beaten. When the unfortunate victim returned to his hut, Goldy came in with a large pair of scissors, cut off his forelock and then slashed him across the face, inflicting a nasty wound.

With Goldy carrying on his persecution our watch system became so organised that it was almost impossible for him to catch anyone unawares. From the very first sighting his movements were flashed around the camp and our scouts never lost sight of him. Nevertheless he was never satisfied until he had hammered some unfortunate even if he just happened to look at him.

Whenever Yoshida was sighted the message 'Flag eight!' went around; the naval flag signal for 'Enemy in sight'. Approval of his methods by the Japanese powers-that-be gained Yoshida rapid promotion. By 1945 he was camp commandant. (Knights of Bushido, Lord Russell of Liverpool: Cassell 1958).

Sometimes nothing much seemed to happen for a while, then suddenly there would be a flurry of activity on the part of the Japs. During one such week the Japs granted permission for the more energetic among us to use the football ground. On the same evening a guard came through our hut and showed us some photographs of the *Exeter*'s dying moments. Then we each received a number and it appeared we were real prisoners now. Mine was E29.

Some of our officers came around the huts taking the names of men who had received technical training and noting the occupations of the men before joining the service. We all feared that something was in the wind and it seemed that technicians would be separated from the non-technical and the camp would break up. Each group pondered on its future while days passed with nothing happening.

'Saturday, April 25th. ... Had to muster again at 0945 and marched to the opposite end of the camp to witness a ceremony by the guard, thirteen in number plus the sergeant and the commandant. They faced north and at a certain time they all saluted for a few seconds (except those who removed their caps in error and had to hurriedly replaced them when they noticed their mistake) and the ceremony was over. There is nothing smart about these Japanese and I still wonder how on earth they have met with such success in the war. I was told later that this was the last day of mourning. Apparently they have been mourning the dead, both their own and those of their enemies for the last three days.'

What we saw of Japanese ceremonial did not impress us; the soldiers always seemed shabby and down at heel. There was none of the crisp efficiency to which we were accustomed. We called it bull but to a certain extent it did give us a feeling of pride in ourselves. It is when it is overdone that it becomes tiresome.

One day a funeral procession went by along the road by the camp. The coffin was preceded by a Japanese soldier carrying a vase of flowers. Eight bearers carried the coffin which seemed to be a bit large for the average Jap. Immediately behind the coffin was another soldier carrying a tray of food which caused a great deal of comment as it would have been much more beneficial to us than the departed Jap.

The emperor's birthday was an occasion I will never forget. We were assembled around a plot of grass to witness the ceremony the Japs put on in celebration. Marching onto the grass they formed two files and faced east. Then removing their hats to expose their cropped heads they bowed and then shambled off.

It wasn't the ceremony that made the occasion memorable.

We spent the whole day without seeing a single grain of rice. the rations comprised boiled beans and potatoes swimming in a thick brown gravy. I went to bed feeling as tight as a drum. In fact I don't think I have ever felt so uncomfortable before. Even taking several turns around the compound failed to afford any relief.

A surprise search caught us all on the hop. As everyone took his meagre belongings outside on to the lawn there was frantic digging and hiding of everything considered illegal. We were formed into a line and searched by the guards whilst a supercilious officer supervised the whole operation. If a prisoner was not standing to attention in the Japanese fashion with fingers stretched—unlike our way with hands clenched and thumb in line with the seam of the trousers—Gold Tooth administered the necessary punishment. When this *[personal search]* was completed we then had to stand by our belongings and as the guard came to search them we had to salute him. My searcher flew into a rage when he saw a Dutch dictionary in my little pile. I was punched in the face and kicked and the dictionary confiscated. Later our Senior Engineer, Lt. Commander Chubb, restored it to me and to avoid a similar incident he advised me to stick a piece of paper on the back with a number written on it so that it looked like a library book. Goldy had a field day as the Dutch were found in possession of tins of corned beef, fruit and butter which were confiscated. He delivered judgment and punishment on the spot. A double-barrel gun was found in the Americans quarters, whilst the poverty-stricken English had the least taken from them and for a time felt smug and self-righteous.

On a different note Ted recorded the brighter side of life as well as the bad in a prison camp.

So many books had now been brought into the camp *[by the working parties]* that an officer had been appointed to allocate them to each hut. Under his librarianship the books were fairly distributed and changed around at regular intervals. Time and again we blessed such writers as Hugh Walpole, A.E.W.Mason, Philip Gibbs, John Buchan, Bartemus, Jeffrey Farnol and a lot of others who lightened our darkest days and helped us retain our sanity.

'Friday 1st May. Wonderfully fresh morning, could well have been England with the incessant chatter of the nesting sparrows and the crowing cocks. Joined up with the PTIs crowd for PT this morning and thoroughly enjoyed it. Standing at the back I was thrilled to watch and participate in such a display of physical training. Brought the breakfast from the galley, obtaining from the chief cook two flattened loaves for myself (my lucky day).

'Edgar was very early this morning and I had a very good lesson. I believe my accent is improving. He seems to think that the big effort in this part of the world will be in June. During the lesson the fragrance of the jasmine blossoms was continually wafted towards us and all around people were whistling as they worked at their routine duties. Altogether I felt in an almost happy frame of mind.

'There was a rather nasty incident that dispelled this feeling of well-being. I couldn't use our lavatories because each one was occupied by Dutch native soldiers so I used the section reserved for Dutch officers. I was immediately rebuked by a huge Dutchman with hate oozing out of his every pore. But I had the satisfaction of showing him his native troops in occupation of our section, so he vented his spleen on them.

'Attended the Afrikaans lesson class for an hour and then the bugle call sounded for dinner. Absolutely no appetite for the rice so I had two cucumber sandwiches—bless you Bill for the extra bread!—this I divided among the cubicle. Spent the afternoon doing my homework and then had a visit from Sam who had just come in from the hospital ship.

'There was much thunder in the afternoon and a few heavy showers which cooled the air beautifully. Supper was rice and egg; How I detest the horrible stuff. But during the evening we were given a large bone straight from the galley on which there were several pieces of meat. So with a piece of bread I did well. Smithy ran the gauntlet and boiled up some coffee and, with Ron and Barry being out we drank it before they returned and the nightly muster came.

'Wonderful sky at sunset with every conceivable hue from black to the very palest of greens. During our walk a big moon rose and shone down on us; a huge yellow moon set in a frame of palm fronds

'Another surprise; was given a block of sugar which should help the rice down.

'Rather interesting yarn on stage illusions before turning in.

'The outside working party brought in some 'news' today:

'1.The allied fleets control the Java Seas and the Jap fleet has been forced to retire to Singapore.

2. The Germans have launched a great offensive in Southern Poland.'

'<u>Thursday 7th May.</u> Up early this morning and whilst washing had the satisfaction of seeing a Jap sentry walk into the barbed wire—I hope he has some sewing to do now. Joined up with Clubs [*Physical Training Instructor*], Taff and Blacky (the pilot) in early morning PT on the dew-drenched grass and in the moonlight and enjoyed it thoroughly. This is the best I've ever felt in the camp.

'No lesson today, did a little on my own account but couldn't settle down as Ron was occupying our only chair. Wonderful morning, felt almost at peace with the world whilst having my beard trimmed.

'Started Radclyff Hall's "The Unlit Lamp" which promises to be entertaining reading.

'Poor Ron has been sent to the isolation ward as his throat is more serious than at first supposed. I know he had a bad night because I awoke several times and heard the the noises from his throat.

'Made great inroads into the midday rice possibly owing to the presence of <u>three</u> pieces of meat.

'What is the matter with me lately? Am I getting older and more irritable, or am I thinking too much of our health? As I was sweeping the grains of rice from our cubicle floor into the passageway outside, the two piles of filth which were heaped one either side of the passage, plus discarded surgical dressings made me wild with rage. There is a dustbin only three yards from our front door and yet they're too lazy to utilise it. The hordes of flies that are attracted are too awful to mention.

'Threatened today by a visit from Prince Chehi Bu(?), a brother of the Mikado. We assembled twice on the roadway without seeing him. Two eggs and a plate of rice per man, so if we didn't see the prince we celebrated.

'Dixie came back from town with the working party and said that while he was working a tiny coloured girl came to him and gave him some native confection "ondie-ondie" and said "Bless you, Mister!". Later a Salvation Army man said covertly to him, "Keep your chin up, the news is good!" so it would appear things are looking up.

'Beautifully starry night with a suspicion of a chill in the air.'

'Few rumours today:

1. Calais and Boulogne have been captured by us.

2. New Guinea, Amboin and another Island are definitely in allied hands.

3. Kobe, Yokohama and Tokyo being bombed incessantly.'

The removal of Ron to the hospital ship *Optenoorte* cast us all down. He had been complaining for several days of a sore throat and finally we made him see Doctor Syred who promptly diagnosed diphtheria. To add to our misfortunes young Jeff contracted a very painful foot. He lay for days in our cubicle without moving and the stench of putrefying flesh became unbearable. The treatment he got was extremely perfunctory so I appealed to my friend Edgar to help us, knowing that he had good relations with the Dutch doctors. Within a short time Jeff was taken to the isolation quarters where he was successfully treated with soda.

Later Ron and Jeff returned to the cubicle the same day. Poor Ron had been stricken with dysentery while in the hospital ship and had barely recovered from this foul complaint when he had to walk the three miles back to the camp. He looked old and weak and spoke with a heavy nasal accent. When he tried to drink, the liquid came from his nose.

Diphtheria raged through the camp and several men in the British compound died. Jeff developed the symptoms and was sent to the hospital ship for treatment. When he returned he looked like an old man and [like Ron] spoke with a heavy nasal accent. It seems that the membrane between the mouth and the nose is destroyed and when he tried to drink anything quickly the liquid came out of his nostrils; or if he tried to blow his lifebelt up the air merely passed out of his nose. He also suffered a partial paralysis which made him almost a cripple.

CHAPTER 3

Macassar II

Ted's journal continues through May as things settled down in the camp with a starvation diet, bad food, dysentery, and beatings; despite which he records a few pleasurable aspects of life. There are still the wildly exaggerated rumours, sometimes based on truth. Madagascar for example, was actually taken in early May. Perhaps the prisoners are sustained by these rumours because there certainly seems to be a feeling that the war will be over in a couple of months. Ted would rather be on a ship seeing it through to the end, as if that end were coming soon. It is as well that they do not know that their incarceration is to last three and a half years. The following are extracts from May and June which give a picture of the everyday life in the camp.

'<u>Friday 8th May.</u>   More PT by moonlight this morning, wonderfully exhilarating to feel the dew on our bare feet. Although I feel well I'm still terribly weak, only being able to do four press-ups.

'The muster roll took so long today that there was no time for the usual mass physical training. My egg was hardly as fresh as could be desired but I risked it. The bread was clean and wholesome and the coffee almost sweet although nearly cold. Altogether a satisfying and for me, the best meal of the day.

'No lesson again today so spent a profitable and interesting forenoon on my own account. Also spent a good time [reading] "The Unlit Lamp" which has made quite an impression on me. A lot of books have been brought into the camp from the deserted houses in the town which will ease the boredom of the present situation for many. Some of the chaps have taken to making such things as moccasins out of spare pieces of cloth; very useful for keeping the pestilential flies off one's feet. Others carve chessmen or cut elaborate decorations on the bamboo cups they make. Yet others make fearsome looking knives and there are all sorts of bamboo spoons in evidence and a few novel ladles fashioned from coconut shells.

'Everyone seems to have settled down to make the best of a

bad job but there are a few who say they prefer this useless life to being on board a ship. Personally I think it's wretched luck being landed like this—I should have loved to be in at the kill, seeing that we have followed the campaign out here from the outset, continuing where the *P.o.W* [*Prince of Wales*] and *Repulse* left off.

'There was a minute portion of fried fish with the rice at dinnertime, which was quite an unsatisfactory meal for me .

'Beautiful sunny afternoon tempered with a fresh breeze. Finished "Unlit Lamp" and then wrote a tentative letter to a prospective employer on my slate. My qualifications looked really convincing. I hope they will stand me in good stead when the time comes.

'That horrible fish and rice again for supper. Was glad to have a crust saved from dinner. Altogether a most unsatisfactory day, thought more than ever of home. I have only to close my eyes to conjure up all the faces of those at home.

'The buzzes are stupendous today:

1. Chinese troops have taken Burma.

2. Heavy bombing on Vlad and also Kobe etc.

3. Russian troops have broken through the German lines on the Latvian Border.

4. We have taken possession of Martinique, Madagascar and New Caledonia from the French.

5. Hitler has paid a visit to his troops on the eastern front to bolster their morale.

'Had our names checked over again by the Japs; this seems to be a monthly practice now.'

'Saturday, 9th. Had a horrible night and a ghastly forenoon; the egg I had yesterday must have caused this. It makes me wild to think that when I have to be fit and strong something crops up and knocks me over. Spread my bed out in the afternoon and tried to sleep it off.

'Edgar came to see me this afternoon. He intends to give me three lessons per week now, as he is teaching Greek to one of his officers who, in his turn is teaching Edgar Japanese. He brought a small cake and a cup of delicious liquid which revived my drooping spirits. He has heard some news which he will not divulge but he is quite confident that things will be moving for us during June and July!

'Tried to sleep off the rest of the day, Taff came to see me and brought some milk. He had great success with the working party today having brought back twelve tins of milk.

'During an inspection of the camp by the Chief MO of the *Optenoorte* a Japanese noticed that one of our fellows had plugged an electric heater into a light socket. The whole cubicle had to report to the guard house and were all severely beaten up with a base ball club. One of the fellows had a bone in his arm broken. But the worst of it all was the fact that there were two boys included in that five and they were as severely beaten as the rest. [*Boy Seamen could be anything from 16 to 18*]

'The Japs are said to have lost 8 cruisers, 18 destroyers and 14 transports on their last attempt on Australia.'

'Sunday 10th. Not much of a night: I'm beginning to dread turning in now because my hip bones ache intolerably when they slide off the life jacket. My knees and feet are as sore as can be where they are in contact with the boards. Spent a better day though, but was all the time conscious of an uneasy feeling inside and afraid to eat or drink anything for fear of the consequences. As I didn't rig the 'squito net last night [I] collected no fewer than 12 bites about the face and hands.

'The 1st Lieutenant mustered us after church today and told us about the floggings and on the whole gave us a very sensible talking to. As far as I understand naval discipline is to be introduced and when he mentioned some of our fellows caught stealing on the hospital ship, I felt really ashamed. When Navvy first started working for us he placed all of us on our honour more or less; but the minority, by which the majority is judged, has badly let Navvy and his successor down.

'Managed to sleep for most of the afternoon, had some soup for supper and spent a very placid evening. Finished reading "Guv'ner", Edgar Wallace and Barny has managed to get "Trader Horn".

'The Rumours today are:
1. The Americans have taken Korea and the inhabitants have declared for the allies.(again!)
2. The British and American fleets have managed to confine the Jap fleet to these waters.'

'Monday 11th Horrid night again. I fully appreciate now how a man can age with this scourge, dysentery. Felt much better during the forenoon and had a much needed wash day. I never wring out my clothing in fresh water as I like to smell the soap in the material when I don my clean shift. Had just finished when Edgar arrived to give me the Dutch lesson. He bore tidings of a battle off the Solomon Islands but with no details. [*Probably Battle of the Coral Sea*]. A word of encouragement regarding my Dutch to English translation was music to my ears. Spent the rest of the day very placidly; padded the arm chair with my pillow and lifebelt.

'Old Taff is down now, seems like malaria. The sooner we're out of this treacherous climate the better I shall be pleased.

'As we had that hated rice again for supper I had to be content with two cucumber sandwiches. During the day I seem to feel fairly well but when mealtimes arrive and I see the rest of the fellows wolfing down their rice, I cannot even look at mine.

'Very sultry evening, appears to be an approaching storm, with the smell of sulphur in the air most noticeable. Lightning very blue and thunder slowly approaching. Rigged the mosquito net tonight as I don't intend to be punished as I was last night. 1st Lt. has made an order that our fellows should remain behind the wire, so we are in prison conditions at last!

'Today's rumours concern enormous Japanese naval losses which I heartily pray are true. They are said to have lost 2 battleships, including a flag ship, 2 aircraft carriers, 8 cruisers, 14 destroyers and 41 transports. Allied losses include 2 aircraft carriers and the *Canberra* but this news is somewhat obscure.

[*Presumably this rumour was based on the Battle of the Coral Sea (4-8 May) in which the Japanese lost one light carrier, one destroyer and some small craft and had one of their six fleet carriers damaged. This against the American loss of one fleet carrier and another damaged and the loss of a destroyer and an oiler. The cruiser HMAS* Canberra *was not present but was to be sunk three months later off Guadalcanal in 'Iron Bottom Sound'; so named by the Americans because of the numbers of ships sunk there.*]

'Monday 18th. Can't say I like our new routine, breakfast at seven makes the day long. The coffee this morning was nearly cold and the egg I saved was bad. But Pedro came to the rescue with a lump of meat which made me crave solid sustenance all the morning.

'Didn't even pretend to work this morning, just stood in the sun. Books were collected later in the afternoon from houses in the town. I had two from the library here; Dutch novels. As I was about to take them from the bookshelf and hand them to one of the boys, the Jap swine [Gold tooth] in charge of the party struck me with his weighted stick. I lost count of the strokes but gave him a demonstration of how an Englishman can take punishment. I can only pray for the day when I can meet him on equal terms when I'll give him something to remember me by. Just recently he had plucked the moustaches from two of our fellows' faces so someone else will be waiting for him too. Played Barny at crib and kept smelling the cloves in the native cigarettes. They reminded me of home and apple tart and cream. Had a walk with the Taffs in the evening but my mind was seething with this morning's happenings.'

'Thursday 28th. A rain-drenched morning, very dull but the promise of a fine day manifest in every sign in the sky. Everywhere the grass looks fresh and the rain or dew deposited so heavily on each blade of grass appears like frost.

'The bread, although whiter in appearance and containing fewer weevils, is barely edible and has a nasty tang. The coffee was however quite decent and above all hot.'

'Friday 29th. No wonder the yesterday's coffee tasted so good, when all the coffee had been drained off one of those giant lizards was found in the copper! No jam for breakfast thanks to R.'s gluttony. He's been at the jam tin several times and, unforgivably, between meals. The bread still possesses a peculiar taste; but still it's bread and not rice, so that's something to be thankful for. Just before muster Taff brought me two slices of meat to make a sandwich for dinner and shortly after brought me a lump of flesh, so my star is very much in the ascendant today. At dinner time Smithy managed to bring along a mug of meat juice which we used on the rice and I shared the meat so the meal was quite good. I had the pleasure of leaving an empty plate for a change.

'Wonderful news this afternoon, Taff from the sick bay saw six allied planes and the bursts of AA fire around them. So at last we are receiving attention and the number seems to indicate that we have a base somewhere out here. Feel tremendously bucked.'

His favourite time of day is in the early morning about which he often becomes quite lyrical. Thus on Sunday 31st May he writes: 'Going for a wash this morning a huge mellow moon was sinking in the sky and in the east the clouds were glowing with the caress of the morning sun.' *But then he goes on to record the rest of the day:* 'One of the Dutchmen died this morning — diphtheria — two of our fellows went sick this morning with sore throats— there is a definite increase and it's looking serious. Went to church this morning but could obtain no comfort today. This type of

Pages from Ted's diary. (Anderson)

chaplain doesn't make much appeal to me. What did touch me however was a little later in the hut when when some of the fellows were singing harvest festival hymns and finished with Blake's "Jerusalem". The rice was again clean and cooked. I only had three maggots and a few weevils and despite the meat being scanty I ate the whole of my ration.'

Each evening he takes a stroll with 'the boys' or else goes over to the 'Taffs' room when they discuss all manner of subjects such as classical music, cooking, what they were going to do when they got home. One serious discussion was whether, on a winter's night is it best to to stick your feet straight down the bed between the cold sheets or to curl up and put them down gradually!

But relations are sometimes strained within the cubicle.

It wasn't long before we began to get on each other's nerves; little gestures and motions became sources of annoyance. Ron used to madden me with his irritating quirk of raising his eyebrows to indicate that he hadn't heard something. He was always ready to contest the least remark whether it was made facetiously or otherwise. Barny had the vexatious habit of saying 'Whaa?' in a most inane manner even when you knew he had heard what he said. Another thing that caused some heated arguments were people who were prepared to watch the others do all the work and not lend a hand themselves. Men who held responsible positions in civilian life could never see when a cubicle needed washing out or when water bottles required filling.

'Friday 12th June. The uncomfortable current of tension came to a head today between Barny and the rest of us. B. told me his feelings towards old Smithy and I asked him if he could swallow his feelings and make allowances for the amount of time we were thrown on each other's company. He replied that making all due allowances, he couldn't possibly overlook his dislike of "Smudge". Just before going to bed the whole thing came to a head and Barny was vehement in his accusations. The whole thing started when there was trouble about the tobacco, when Bandy and Smithy were at the mercy of Barny and Jeff. Apparently he [Barny] thought that Bandy and Smudge had been too lavish in their expenditure but instead of saying what he thought at the time and clearing the air, he has brooded on it ever since until the whole affair has attained such gigantic proportions [in his mind] that he really believes he has a genuine grievance. The effect on him has been very noticeable and I have seen him gradually withdraw into his shell, rarely speaking to anyone and causing quite an uncomfortable feeling between us all,

'That's the curse of prison life, each petty grievance becomes enormously magnified, with frayed tempers, hot words and little chance of escape from each other in these confined quarters. The only answer is enormous tolerance but unfortunately people of Barny's stamp regard tolerance as a sign of weakness and violent quarrels can break out, while others just brood and become miserable.

'Had the evening walk with Tommy. Quite a pleasant evening but the mosquitoes were out in force even penetrating the socks on one's feet. Our conversation tonight was chiefly on matrimony. Had a most welcome invite to beef tea which was really fine. I owe my recovery [from dysentery] and gradually increasing strength to this "witch's brew" as the Chief Mech. calls it. Continued our discussion until well past 2130 when, returning to the cubicle, was just in time to witness the stormy row.

'The mornings still continue to be cold so I go to bed with a green coat (about two sizes too big, thus offering extra warmth) over my blue shirt. Then I tuck my overall trousers into my socks and I'm ready for sleep.

'Regarding socks, I suppose I must be considered one of the most affluent men in the camp. I have five all told, a pair I brought with me from the ship and three which Bandy gave me. Their mosquito-proof qualities are negligible but the psychological effect on morale is tremendous!'

'Saturday 4th July. The row which has been brewing again in the cubicle came a step nearer when Ron and Barny had a few words. Fortunately I missed this, being away assisting Taff with the sick quarters coffee. But Barny is a selfish person; I had noticed it on the hospital ship and I doubt there will be any harmony in our cubicle while he is there. On the other hand, although Ron is still groggy he makes little effort to help himself, which makes me wild. I hardly think it necessary for a young man to remain inside four walls 23 out of 24 hours a day, even though he is still suffering from the after effects of malaria, especially when he complains of coldness in his hands and feet and there is a glorious sun just outside.'

'Thursday 16th July. There was a wonderful fight in the Coconut Grove this afternoon, a "grudge fight" which was the outcome of an argument last night. The two contestants were well matched, both accused and the accuser having a good knowledge of boxing. Justice was meted out with the accused knocking out the accuser in the third round of a fine fight in which the fortunes were always wavering from one side to the other.' (Grudge fights were always settled in Coconut Grove with the gloves but considering the conditions in which we now lived these were surprisingly few.)

Although fighting was a punishable offence in the Royal Navy, a 'grudge fight' was an excellent and semi-official way of relieving the tensions of living in confined quarters in a ship. The matter was settled with a scratch boxing match on the forecastle refereed by somebody such as a petty officer or leading hand and witnessed by a crowd of eager onlookers. After three generally ineffective rounds in well-padded boxing gloves, honour was satisfied and the adversaries shook hands, often becoming the best of friends thereafter.

It was generally accepted by everyone that it would be practically impossible to escape from the camp for many reasons, the chief of which was betrayal by the natives who were notorious for their treachery. So when the news broke that three Dutchmen had escaped the whole camp seethed with excitement. It was difficult to imagine how they expected to get away with it because they were disliked by the natives due to their harsh colonial policies. A whole day went by without any move on the part of the Japs and then at five o'clock in the evening we were mustered on the roadway. After waiting for over an hour six Japanese soldiers with fixed bayonets accompanied by an officer subjected us to a rigorous search. Our cubicles were then searched and our few belongings scattered all over the hut. As it was evident that whatever the Japs were searching for was not to be found in the British quarters we were dismissed and allowed to try and restore some order in our huts. The Dutch community had much of their property confiscated and also had to surrender their swords. For some reason the Americans came in for disapproval as four of them were thrown into cells and the Indonesians, caught skylarking by Goldy, were ordered to line up in two ranks facing each other and slap each others faces until told to stop. During all this Goldy's face was crinkled in a permanent grin, slit eyes even narrower and the radiance of his gold teeth was blinding as he savoured the situation to the full.

The search lasted until seven o'clock, just as the three Dutchmen were brought in through the gate. They were heavily bound and had been badly beaten up. Later we learned that, as we suspected, they had been betrayed by the natives.

There were various repercussions following the escape. All the Dutch had to have their hair cropped; they were not allowed to play football and were barred from the canteen. The whole camp had to hand in all money. 30,000 guilders were collected from the Dutch army personnel. The amount from their navy was not disclosed, although we had always thought that the sailors were fabulously rich. Goldy liked the idea of close-cropped heads so he decided that the British should cut their hair as well. Our barbers worked feverishly to complete our shearing by the deadline next day. On the Sunday following, the chaplain's sermon was based on the text; 'His hair shall grow again'.

The same day turned out to be eventful because at 4.30 we had to muster on the basketball pitch, then after much confusion arising from misunderstanding among the Japs and frantic antics from Goldy, we were marched to the Coconut Grove. After waiting for an hour a car drew up and a Japanese officer got out. This personage was the great Mori and, standing on a platform he began to read in execrable English a proclamation saying the three Dutchmen had been found guilty and were sentenced to death by shooting. The authorities were satisfied that their cubicle mates were not involved so they would be punished less severely with solitary confinement for three months.

The day had not yet finished because we were then marched off to undergo a medical inspection by Jap doctors under the supervision of Mori and his gold braided staff. After the medical they then took particulars of our names, ships, next of kin, where sunk and other details that should have been registered at the start of our captivity.

On the same day one of our shipmates died of malaria despite the efforts of our doctors to save him, hampered as they were by the lack of facilities.

It is not clear who this Mori was as Ted also writes of another one later on. There are three mentioned by Lord Russell in Knights of Bushido, *two of whom could have been in this area. One was a sergeant, in mentality the double of Yoshida. Another was an admiral who, at a luncheon given for him, regaled his fellow-guests with tales of cannibalism in the Sino-Japanese war whilst they ate the liver of Lt. Hall USAAF.*

About this time Ted went out on one of the working parties.

For some weeks I worked on the road which was being constructed at Maros, near the aerodrome. This involved a journey of about twenty miles in a lorry, passing through the suburbs [where there were] lovely houses and gardens all spoiled by the hated symbol of the rising sun flag all over the place. It was even hung behind the altars of some of the churches we passed on the way. There was one solitary German flag outside a house; the only one I saw throughout the war.

The site of the road was on a plateau surrounded by mountains which faded into the blue of the distance. All day gorgeous butterflies and graceful swallows would be flying around us. Sometimes Jap fighter planes would come over in practice dogfights; but in spite of our hopes they never crashed.

About four hundred of us worked in the broiling sun stripped to the waist, which reminded me of a scene from the film 'Suez'. We were not driven hard at first and were allowed yasumés under a canvas awning three or four times a day. Water was provided in large tin drums placed on either side of the road from which we drank with a large wooden ladle. Enterprising natives conducted clandestine business from the bushes by the road, selling arrow-root and eggs. By far the best buy was the native sugar—gula-java. Shaped like a torpedo and dark brown in colour it was very sweet and could make the most unpalatable rice acceptable.

On work of this kind it was quite easy to appear to be working hard yet actually make no great effort. The most tolerant guard we had was called 'Handlebars' because of his luxuriant moustache. He told us that his wife and children had been interned in America and he was praying for the day when they would be re-united. He was really good to us; but later on when the Japs thought the work was not proceeding quickly enough they stood over us with sticks the whole of the day. Sometimes they put young boys of barely sixteen over us and these sadistic little monsters barely let up with their sticks. In spite of this I enjoyed the work outside and on arrival back at camp in the evenings I would swill down with water, have supper and go to bed. I never remember my head touching the pillow during those days.

To reward our efforts we were allowed a rest day every fifth day and we would return to the camp the evening before as happy as schoolboys. One day our return coincided with the arrival of a Japanese big noise and we were ordered to double away out of sight. As we hurried away we left a trail of gula java, eggs and arrowroot as they fell from poacher's pockets in the panic. Oddly enough nothing was ever said about it.

But these comparatively pleasant days were soon to end.

'<u>Wednesday, 2nd August</u>. After a day of horrible food (the bread and coffee at breakfast being the high spot of the day) we were shaken out of our normal routine by the ERAs, OAs, EAs, shipwrights, carpenters and joiners having their names taken. Eighty are required from the English contingent, thirty from the American, 600 from the Dutch navy and 100 from the army. Up to now mechs have not been mentioned, thank goodness! I am not keen to leave here because the nature of the work is not yet known and we should have to start camp life all over again. Speaking to Bandy in the evening he told me that the Dutch colonel says nothing will come of this. But I wonder how much longer this life is going to continue.'

'<u>Thursday 3rd</u>. —the names of the English going on this mysterious job for the Japs have been promulgated and up to now my name has not been mentioned.'

'<u>Friday 4th</u>. My relief was very much short-lived as the names submitted by our people have been rejected by the Japs, who have compiled their own list which includes my name. All the ERAs, OAs and shipwrights are going with the exception of the boiler-makers. There are two sorts of conjecture regarding our future; but personally I think we are just being moved out of the way. Our engineer officers are also included.'

Work as far as the segregated members of the technical party were concerned finished when each man was kitted out with a pair of gym shoes, two singlets, two pairs of cotton shorts, two pairs of socks, two thin blankets and two sailor suits. The shorts and singlets were far too small for any of us. These last were of the type worn by Lascars and no doubt had been looted from the *Optenoorte*.

The Japanese 'number one man' [the petty officer in charge of the party] then took us under his wing. Every day he took us for physical training and games and for a Jap he was quite tolerant and pleased with our efforts. We learnt sufficient Japanese to obey orders on the march but there was also a Dutchman called Budding who acted as interpreter. He was in fact the regular interpreter who had been employed in a Japanese bank before the war and had acquired a good knowledge of the language.

Budding imparted any information that the Japs gave out to the prisoners; but obviously not very satisfactorily as far as the British were concerned.

When he had any information to give us he would tell us in ten minutes what took him about half an hour to tell his fellow countrymen; thus we only knew that a sea journey was imminent when the Dutch came around our quarters trying to buy our life belts, for which they offered large sums of money. But no Dutch money could buy my old belt; it had almost literally become a part of me.

The first lieutenant, anticipating our departure, came round to cheer us up. He also suggested that if there came an opportunity to do a little sabotage we should seize it. From then on we were in a continual state expectancy, living each day as it came without thinking of the next.

Under the tutelage of Mori [*the number one man*] we continued to practice our drill on the football pitch and, stripped to the waist we became as brown as the Indonesians. As he never flew into a rage like his fellows did it was quite pleasant and kept our minds occupied.

About this time the Jap who was in charge of the galley acquired an Alsatian which he set upon the now increasing cat population of the camp. Shortly after I had seen this animal seize a cat and kill it instantly, it bit Goldy in the calf, which bit of news flashed delightedly around the camp. Goldy however vented his spleen on our first lieutenant on the pretext that he had allowed the English working parties to leave the camp in ragged clothes!

There also followed one of the worst examples of brutality to occur in the camp so far when Goldy and a few of his chums set upon an Indonesian. He was beaten with a baseball bat until he collapsed, then the whole gang jumped upon him, stamping on him with their iron shod boots. Finally his hair was burnt off and he was tied to the camp gate for the night.

Ted does not say what became of him afterwards. Presumably the victim survived.

We knew that our stay in Macassar was ending when the Nips wanted to know if any of us had attache cases, rather as if they thought that like the Dutch we had walked off the ship fully packed up. Then on a brilliant day Mori gave us our 'passing out' parade in the presence of a diminutive Jap who obviously was of some importance as he was treated with great deference by the camp Nips who bowed to him on every possible occasion. The parade over, he handed us over to the camp commandant who spoke at length and concluded by giving us a packet off cigarettes each. Obviously it had been a great success.

Having been given a Dutch army haversack each to carry our belongings we assembled on the football pitch ready to go, in a fog of secrecy and gnawing uncertainty as to our destination.

The Dutch colonel came around and wished us goodbye and we marched off as our first lieutenant stood at the gate to see us on our way. we were sorry to leave him behind and we wondered if we would ever have such a champion for our wellbeing as we had had in him. As we walked to the jetty—a far more comfortable journey from that to the camp with blistered feet—the guards who accompanied us rode on bicycles and slashed importantly at the native onlookers as they passed.

Before we embarked we were addressed by a nasty little officer who wished us a good voyage and good health. He said that we were going to a fair city and that we should be well treated. On which note the 250 strong English contingent was bundled down into the hold at the very bottom of the ship, where we lay or sat on the straw that covered the steel plates; packed like sardines—a well worn cliche but very apt in the circumstances. As we sat, there was a sudden vibration and the familiar sound of diesel engines firing and we left for our unknown destination in the MS *Osama Maru*.

CHAPTER 4

Koyaki Jima

Immediately I stepped off the ladder below I was enveloped in an overpowering claustrophobia and it was difficult to ward off the incipient panic. But I lay back and closed my eyes and gradually my senses returned to normal.

With little ventilation, the heat was intense and as the breathing of 250 souls further polluted the atmosphere it was worsened by the stench of perspiration. All night I used my enamel plate as a fan and listened to the snores of those fortunate enough to be able to sleep. At one time I happened to glance at Chief Mechanician Bennett who was sleeping peacefully beside me; and as I looked a creature about the size of a mouse scuttled across his face with a horrible rustling noise. Several times in the night as I fell asleep I was awakened by one of these loathsome creatures running across my throat and face. [*Probably cockroaches of which there are some large species in the Pacific area*]

The food, although not plentiful was considerably better than at Macassar. It was far cleaner and more wholesome. Sometimes we were allowed on the upper deck for quarter hour periods, which was a taste of paradise compared with down below. The cool sea air seemed to cleanse us of the vileness of the hold that nevertheless was waiting for us after our temporary reprieve. One day we spent the whole forenoon on the upper deck and the cool air relieved the prickly heat [heat rash] which by now covered most of us from head to foot. On the way back to the hold we passed the cabins occupied by the Dutch and Indonesians which seemed to many of us an insult. What had their war effort amounted to? Hadn't they folded up as soon as Jerry stepped over their border? Didn't a Dutch destroyer surrender to a Japanese minesweeper?

We were allowed the use of a wash place but it was difficult to get in at all because the Indonesians were always there playing a hose over each other. Frustration overcame our reason and several bitter fights broke out.

In this wash place the Japs had two enormous lizards in boxes, Komodo dragons fully eight to ten feet in length. Long before you reached the wash place you caught their vile smell. It was quite impossible for them to move within the confines of their boxes; they seemed to be carved from stone and there was not so much as a blink of an eyelid to indicate a sign of life. They were fed daily with live fowls through a hatch at the end of the box. Sometimes the unfortunate bird would cringe for a long time in a corner before the monster would suddenly seize its meal. There followed an alarmed squawk, a shower of feathers and the dragon would assume its immobility to digest its food. We envied these creatures their meal for it would have been nice to swap some of our rice for a slice of chicken.

On the evening of the seventh day our senior engineer, Lieutenant Commander Chubb, told us that the 'fair city' to which we were sailing was Nagasaki [*on the southern Japanese island of Kyushu*] and that we were to be employed in a shipyard. Nobody had heard of the place except one character who came up with a line from a silly poem:

'.....natives of Nagasaki, where the people chew tobaccy.'

That evening we had just settled down for another night in our grim quarters when, with frightening suddenness, panic broke out among us. Running into heavy seas the ship had given a violent lurch causing the timbers on the sides of the ship to fall into the hold with a terrifying crash. A voice screamed, 'We've been torpedoed!'

Immediately 250 men with one thought uppermost in their minds stampeded for the two ladders, one at each end of the hold. Men who fell were trampled underfoot, those on the ladders were pulled down by others attempting to get on. At the foot of each ladder was a confused mass of fighting bodies; the shouting and screaming was deafening. Then as quickly as it had started the tumult ceased and the men began to look at each other sheepishly. The ship's side was intact, no water was gushing into the hold; we were safe. Gradually we all returned to a state of normality but we had all been badly scared.

During the night the temperature dropped considerably in the hold which relieved the irritation from prickly heat and next morning we dropped anchor in Nagasaki. When, after what we called breakfast we went on the upper deck, it was bitterly cold. Having come in one week from the tropics it struck through the thin clothes we were wearing. We boarded a small boat for the last part of our journey but as we were passing a shipyard the guards most secretively drew the curtains across the windows, a curious action considering we were going to work in one; but from what I was able to see of the scenery it reminded me of Norway.

The boat drew up alongside a jetty on to which we disembarked, where on landing just before us, the Dutch had dropped their luggage. The Japs insisted that we should carry it for them and, our protests at this final insult being quite useless, after a few blows with rifle butts we were forced to do as we were told. The injustice of it all was overwhelming as we had only haversacks for our belongings whereas the Dutch had kitbags. Due to their hitherto ample diet, they were in immeasurably better condition than us and yet we had to carry their stuff as well as our own. However the Japs did not seem to mind when, instead of carrying the bags we dragged them along the ground. As we had to go over some rough ground for about a mile, by the time we reached our destination the kit bags were worn through and most of their contents were left strewn along the path. We dropped the tattered bags at their destination with great satisfaction.

After this we were halted on a bare patch of earth which was surrounded on all sides by soldiers with rifles and bayonets at the ready. It looked quite dramatic and reminded me of a scene from a war film. Facing us was a raised platform on which were seated a number of solemn faced Japs, one of whom got to his feet and in heavy nasal tones told us that we were in Japan to work. The expressions on the faces of the welcoming committee conveyed the impression that he wasn't funning either.

'The next time I see you, I will be able to tell you that the war is over.' he concluded.

Following our reception we were marched to our future home which consisted of a number of wooden buildings set around the edge of a rectangle. But before we were allowed in, our belongings were searched and we had to remain outside in the biting wind for five hours whilst each individual was searched.

The buildings were divided into rooms and were far from finished, there being neither doors nor ceilings and the concrete floors were still wet. Around the rooms were two platforms for sleeping on, the lower one being about two and a half feet above floor level with the upper four feet above that; each platform designed to take fourteen of the fifty six men in each room. Across the width of the room was a long table with a stool along each side not big enough however to accommodate everyone at once.

One of the first formalities we went through was signing and thumb printing a form promising we would not attempt to escape. No one knew whether the Japs had signed the Geneva convention *[amongst other things, recognising the duty of all prisoners of war to escape]* but escape was out of the question anyway. The camp was on an island, built on what was obviously reclaimed land—some estimated about five to seven miles from the town of Nagasaki. Even if one did manage to get off the island to the mainland it was hardly likely that any Nip would help an escaped prisoner. It would also be impossible to move unnoticed as a European would stand out like a wart on a nose.

[It would seem that the Japanese were not that perceptive because a little while later the prisoners were given: '—a green suit made of a coarse hessian-like material with a broad red stripe across the back at shoulder height. These were issued to distinguish us from the Japs.'*]*

For a week we did nothing and occupied our time wandering around visiting friends in other huts and trying to keep warm. With the relentless cold the days seemed to be infinitely longer than at Macassar. Our diet included some palatable bread at first but supplies soon dried up and we settled down to a mixture of rice, barley and small fish dished out whole and complete with eyes. We were also given what looked like slightly coloured water with a few large leaves floating in it. Later this deteriorated into plain water strongly flavoured with putrid fish, because the little fish were actually kept in the tubs into which the water was put at mealtimes.

It was a great relief when we were marched to what we called the square, where we had stopped on our way to the camp. Here speeches were made by a sickly looking naval officer who was in charge of the shipyard where we were going to work. After he had finished, the head man of the yard, a Baron Kawaname, explained what was expected of us and we were then grouped into various working parties. I became a member of the plate markers party and we returned to camp with the message ringing in our ears of 'Hard work and plenty of it. Heavy mortification for slackness or disobedience.'

The next day we mustered again on the square and stood around until noon when we were given a bread roll, which had to be held in the hand at the ready until the interpreter, a supercilious little man, gave the signal to eat. More speeches followed and we were told that if we worked hard the time would pass quickly, five years seeming like two—and we would have wives!

While on the square we saw another Jap addressing a crowd of young Nips. He read his speech from a long roll that looked like a toilet roll. Reading as usual from right to left before long there was quite a length fluttering in the breeze.

Next day we marched to work in groups, each being led by a man carrying a board bearing the party's number and its type of work—welding, rivetting, cutting, caulking and so on. At full strength we numbered about a thousand and, with my party bringing up the rear, when we reached the top of the hill leading down to the dockyard we could see the whole work force, looking like a long sinuous line of ants.

Our first impressions of the shipyard were not favourable as it was still being built but it looked as if it would be a fair sized place when completed. There were four ships of about 8,000 tons resting on blocks in the docks with another being fitted out at the sea wall.

We arrived just in time to see the little ceremony with which the Japs began their working day. Gathering outside their various places of work they turned to the east, bowed several times under the direction of their bosses, replaced their curious jockey-caps and finished with several shouts of 'Banzai!' [*Literally meaning 'Ten thousand years!', the Japanese battle cry implies a willingness to die for the emperor.*]

There were not many grown men working in the yard, most of the work being done by the teenaged lads whose induction we had seen. They lived in wooden huts by the square, which we referred to as Boys Town, and were thoroughly regimented, their lives being regulated by bugle calls. They were almost as much prisoners as we were but were allowed one day a week from work when they journeyed into Nagasaki to enjoy its attractions. They would return from these jaunts worn out and lethargic, the girls and saki having exacted a heavy toll on their physical resources.

We got our mid-day meal, which consisted of two rice balls wrapped in wooden shavings, from a hut in the yard. According to its size each party was allocated one or more buckets of the hot brownish water with the large leaves, which was apparently Japanese green tea. This was our liquid refreshment and we drank it from the large wooden ladles supplied with each bucket. It was invariably tainted with fish but we assumed that as it had been boiled it was safe to drink. The Nip workmen carried their mid-day meal in wooden boxes and they ate their rations at high speed. The box was held up to the mouth and the rice pushed in at a fearsome rate with chopsticks. Eating seemed to be regarded as an irksome necessity from which they derived no enjoyment.

One of the most irritating features of our days was the

interminable counting to which we were subject by the navy or the army before either service would take over responsibility from the other. Sometimes when the process had gone on longer than usual the Japanese navy officers would cast loose among our own officers in their frustration.

The guards counted the prisoners in fives then worked out their sums with sticks in the dirt, or by tracing the figures in the air with their fingers. Only when both sets of figures, dirt or aerial derived, agreed would they take over from the other service. Before the first week was out most of the prisoners were, to say the least, disenchanted with work.

The plate marking job was not too strenuous and consisted of punching centre marks in the plates. The marked plates were then passed to the drillers who drilled the holes which in time would accommodate the rivets. The weather however was bitterly cold, especially in the afternoon when the wind increased with chilling intensity. Even though I wore every stitch of clothing I possessed I still felt like an icicle. The cold from the steel plates, on which we had to squat to do the job, came up through our flimsy footwear into the very marrow of our bones. We tried stuffing paper or straw into our shoes but we could not keep our feet warm. The unnatural squatting position in which we had to work made our thighs ache. Walking to work when the square and paths were reduced to sticky mud by the rain our shoes were sucked off our feet, much to the amusement of the guards. These flimsy gym shoes soon wore out and new ones promised by the Japs were so long in coming that many of our men had to remain in camp as they had nothing to put on their feet. When the 'boots' finally did arrive they turned out to be rubber soles with black cloth uppers, having a separate compartment for the big toe which gave the impression of cloven hooves.

A dry dock was being constructed next to the plate marking area and at 0900 and 1500 blasting took place. This gave us a respite from work twice a day when we had to take cover and was also useful for gauging the time; but we also had several narrow escapes from flying rocks which demolished the roof under which we sheltered.

At night we returned to camp tired and cold to be welcomed by a cold mess of rice. There was always a scramble to get hold of the solitary bucket of water which was provided for each hut to enable fifty-six men to wash. The universal ambition was to get washed before supper so that we could curl up under our blankets and get warm before the evening inspection. We then had to stand to attention while we were counted and remain there with the icy blast blowing through our doorless hut until the whole camp was accounted for.

When we were presented with an old army greatcoat each we could not have been more thrilled because with it we could make quite a snug little bed. There were numberless experiments to determine the most satisfactory way of making a bed on the bare boards. An 'envelope' style was finally deemed the best which we made up carefully with blankets and coat, crawling in and taking care not to stick our feet out at the end; otherwise you had to get out and start all over again.

We tried to wear our greatcoats under our clothes going to work but the Japs decreed that they were to be worn in the camp only and to be detected would mean a flogging. However we were all so numbed by the cold that even the most timid soon risked wearing his coat under his hessian suit.

In time the promised wash place materialised and consisted of a rectangular concrete trough about twenty-five feet by twenty and two and a half feet high. This was filled with cold water which had to be dipped out with wooden basins. As there were 900 men and only fifty basins supplied, inevitably fights broke out between our boys and the Dutchmen; the latter always hogging anything that was going. Every day there would be a milling crowd around the trough all with the same thought, to be washed before supper.

Not surprisingly dysentery and pneumonia took a heavy toll during the first few months. The first coffin, a plain wooden box, to be carried out of the camp while we all stood to attention contained the body of a Dutchman. The spectacle of a wisp of bunting pathetically draped over the coffin was extremely moving. One of the boy seamen in my room was ill for weeks with pneumonia and he lay motionless on the bare boards of his bench a makeshift pillow we had made for him under his head. That he survived and recovered was due in no small way to Dr. Syred, a young English naval doctor who had just finished his training before joining up. He had no drugs or medicines to give but his constant attention and personal care, making the boy's 'bed' and arranging the pillow, helped in no small way to pull him through.

The provision of doors and ceilings to our huts added to our comfort. At night with the doors and windows closed and all the smokers puffing furiously it became very cosy if a bit smoky by inspection time.

Work in the yard was fraught with danger and we had to be

constantly on the alert so as not to be caught out by the carelessness of the Nips. It was therefore everyone's ambition to get a job in the camp but the interpreter Budding saw to it that all these jobs went to the Dutchmen. They also had the all the best jobs in the yards. I tried to get into the drawing office but the Dutchman in charge told me I was too young; I was thirty one at the time. The more I saw of the Dutchmen the more convinced I was that they were prepared to lick the hand which struck them.

When the Nips promised us warm clothes and actually took our measurements, we thought the gates of heaven were to be opened for us. There was also the promise of bread to replace the eternal rice. Promises flowed like the rising tide and we in our ignorance thought they were sincere and paradoxically, despite their non-fulfilment they helped us in spirit at least through a particularly unpleasant period of our captivity.

It was interesting to see the difference in working techniques that the Nips used compared to our own. The Japanese saws used in the yard had teeth on both edges of the blade which was attached to a round handle and when a workman was sawing wood the cut was made by drawing the saw towards him as did the carpenters when using a plane.

In all the shipyards I had seen hitherto ships were built on slipways and at the launching ceremony the chocks were knocked away and the ship glided with increasing momentum down the slipway into the water. In the Japanese yard the ships were built on blocks at the bottom of a dry dock and when she was ready the dock would be flooded and the ship floated out to a nearby jetty for fitting out.

The workmanship was particularly shoddy. When, for example, a gas cutter took too much metal from a steel plate, an electric welder welded the piece back on again. If the rivet holes were not in line the gas cutter burned out the holes so that the rivets could get through. Often they were so much out of line that the rivets went in at all angles and the platers sprang the plates in order to bolt them together. Looking at the results we wondered how their ships could face up to the pounding of heavy seas when almost every rivet in them was under tension. Similarly we wondered what their tanks and aircraft were like.

The Japs liked to make as much noise as possible as they worked no doubt thinking it made for efficiency, the plate markers with whom we worked being some of the worst culprits. The plates were marked for drilling using a wooden template and a long metal punch and hammer. One sharp blow would have been enough but the Japs would strike the steel plate half a dozen times before they hit the punch. It was the same with the riveters who banged away on both plate and rivet with their hammers, so that when we were all working the noise used to ring in our ears long after we had finished.

The way in which materials were misused was startling. Concrete was made up so unsubstantially that it flowed like water and the paint they used was very thin. Their uses of cast iron would have made an engineer shudder. We got the impression that they were very short of materials and were striving to get the maximum production from the minimum materials and labour, both of which seemed to be of very inferior quality. We were highly critical of everything Japanese, exulting when anything went wrong, which it often did, and getting punished for our barely concealed delight.

The Japs seemed to be unaware of any ideas of safety and they took fearsome risks with slender slings which they greatly over-loaded with the result that they snapped, killing and injuring those below. Gas cutters working on high would start cutting without a warning shout to those below, deluging everyone with molten metal and causing a stampede to avoid the lethal shower. Platers dropped nuts, bolts and washers on to prisoners heads deliberately, a pastime that gave them much pleasure.

The death toll in the yard was very high, on average four Nips being killed each week. They took fearful risks and paid the penalty. The hospital, situated just outside the gates always had a full quota of people in plaster or walking around with their arms in cages or else lying in bed, their legs suspended above them.

Sanitation in the yard was crude, consisting of pits over which wooden floors were fitted with holes cut through the wood at intervals. Each hole was separated from its neighbours by a partition and had a door. Everyone including the women used these toilets. When the pits were full they were emptied by Korean women and the stench was noticeable from a hundred yards and could even be smelled when we returned to the camp at night. The contents of the pits were highly prized by the locals as a fertiliser.

From this time on our lives degenerated into a continual round of hunger, filth and weakness. We were given just enough food to keep us alive and be able to work. A good many of our chaps would eat their dinner portion with their breakfast to have the satisfaction of feeling reasonably full at least once a day. This temporary satisfaction was however off-set by a long wait of twelve hours until the next meal. Owing to lack of vitamins a terrible skin disease broke out all over our bodies, some people being so tormented that they scratched the skin from their bodies.

With the arrival of another three hundred English, American and Dutch prisoners, the Dutch senior officer lost his position to a Major Horrigan of the American air force who seemed a worthy champion for us and appeared not to give a hoot for the Japs.

Our plating party was disbanded after a time and most of us were incorporated into the machine erector party which meant that we would have to work in the engine and boiler rooms of the ships being fitted out. At this time of the year it was a better job than being out in the open. My companion on this job was Chief Machinist Johnson of the US Navy, a quiet elderly man who absolutely hated the Japs. But his sane opinions and constant comradeship were always a source of comfort to me. '1944 will be our year, Ted.' he would say; and I hoped his prediction would be correct as I thought that that year would see the limit of my endurance.

Our 'boss' was a small man, cruel and ruthless whose sole aim was to extract the maximum effort from his weak and starving charges. One day when he was more exacting than usual, Johnny said, 'One day Sokato, I'm going to bang you on the head so hard that you'll be bowlegged for the rest of your life, you slant-eyed little bastard!'

Sokato was well aware of the sentiment in Johnny's remark and although he could not understand, he responded with oily maliciousness. All the heavy, dirty jobs fell to Johnny and being his companion to me as well. One of the worst jobs was in the bilges of a ship which were always full of stinking water which we knew to be urine because the Japs never used the lavatories. Sokato put a tiny boy of thirteen to watch over us who reported everything we touched and did. This little urchin swaggered about with the importance of having two 'horreos' (prisoners) under him and I began to know what a tame dancing bear must have felt like.

The (civilian) Nips always held the threat over our heads of reporting us to the kaiguns (Japanese sailors). These navy guards were were far more brutal than the army and beat senseless anyone who fell into their clutches. When we first began working in the shipyard the navy was solely responsible for us. The two elderly guards who were allocated to each working party were fairly rational men who regarded us with a certain amount of awe. They were flattered when we gave them the occasional salute. Unfortunately they were replaced by a younger and more vicious set who we got to know by their particular brands of punishments and all of whom we gave identifying nicknames. One who we dubbed Twinkletoes was a fat sullen youth whose feet made an angle of 180 degrees. He would fly into paroxysms of rage on the least pretext and belabour his victim with both fists on both sides of the face. Anyone too tall for him was made to bend forward so that he could reach. Patcheye was offended if anyone looked at him and he would kick out anywhere on the body. Babyface or the Jockey was a diminutive brat, notorious for his evil temper whose forte was snooping. He could ferret out loafing prisoners from the most unexpected hideouts.

The Mad Mullah's speciality was selecting victims for punishment from the marching ranks as we came through the dockyard gates in the morning. Once inside we all had to run the gauntlet of kaiguns who were stationed on both sides of the road about fifty yards apart. It was their duty (or pleasure) to collect a number of prisoners to provide entertainment for their fellows and for the hundreds of workmen who gathered to watch the prisoners being beaten. The penalty for being out of step, for looking to the right or left instead of straight ahead, or even looking on the ground was to be hauled out of the ranks by the Mad Mullah and marched to the kaigun's hut. Here Chiefy, the chief petty officer in charge administered his ritual beatings. With great ostentation he would pick out a baseball bat, spit on his hands and try it for weight with a few tentative swings in true Lou Gerig fashion. Finding the bat to his liking and having achieved the necessary concentration he would signal that he was ready to start. The victim was made to stand in front of him with his hands stretched above his head while he applied 'heavy mortification', lifting his left foot off the ground to give added impetus to the strokes. The severity of the punishment varied with Chiefy's mood and how the war was going.

In spite of their innate sadism the Japs admired courage, so it was always a good policy to accept floggings without flinching and a gross mistake to expect pity from them. A Dutchman after receiving the first blow fell sobbing to the ground. If he expected mercy he was soon disabused, for Chiefy went berserk and began kicking his victim in the face, stomach, kidneys; anywhere as long as it hurt. The Dutchman was then held up and beaten with the base ball bat until the chief was exhausted. The poor fellow then knelt and begged not to be beaten any more and his plea was answered by another burst of frenzied brutality. The Japanese spectators including women and children who witnessed this savagery where highly delighted and showed their appreciation in no uncertain manner whilst the Dutchman earned from us the name 'The Praying Dutchman'.

Fortunately I was only selected once to provide the entertainment. I was marching in step with the rest of the company, looking straight ahead without blinking my eyes and swinging my arms smartly just as if I were on the parade ground. Yet despite my perfection I was pulled from the ranks by a horrible little brown man. Outside the kaiguns hut various nationalities were segregated. As I watched the little beasts indulging in their bestiality my heart fell down to my boots. I could bear pain but the thought of mutilation or of permanent injury was deeply disturbing. When it came to my turn Chiefy grunted at me. Guessing the meaning of the noise I raised my hands above my head and tensed myself. He walked around me with the baseball bat in his hand. As I noted his features I thought it would be rather good if he had a sudden heart attack or lightning suddenly pierced his objectionable body. But nothing like that happened as I well knew when the first blow caught me squarely across the bottom. A thick cloud of dust arose from my trousers which must surely have indicated that I was a loafer; good workers do not sit down. To stifle any sound I clenched my jaws and held them firmly locked. Five times the bat landed on my backside in exactly the same spot then with another grunt Chiefy indicated that he had finished. As I walked away I knew I would not be able to sit for days but that was nothing to the permanent injury others had suffered through these beatings. With feeling returning to my nether regions I had to walk stiff-legged as normal walking was too painful. But I was pleased that they hadn't realised the significance of the dust clouds from my trousers otherwise I would not have been able to walk at all.

If the hancho of a work party was not satisfied with the work of one of his prisoners he would take the offender to the kaigun's hut where the duty petty officer would listen to the hancho's evidence and deliver judgment and punishment on the spot. Needless to say the prisoner was never in the right.

The navy also kept the Japanese workmen under strict control and would never fail to punish slackers. One day a grown Nip with whom I was working was caught smoking by a kaigun. There was a look of abject terror on his face as the Kaigun searched around for a suitable weapon with which to administer punishment. The Nip, himself a zealous tormenter of prisoners, burst into tears.

There were also the police who had little to do with us at first, their duty being to keep the Japanese at work. They were very zealous and scrambled into every nook and cranny in search of tardy workmen, often getting covered from head to foot with filth in the process. The Nips called them 'Mungies' a name we soon learnt, and it paid us to escape their attention as much as it did the Nips.

Newly recruited policemen had nothing to distinguish them from any other workman except a white armband inscribed with red characters. This enabled them to mix with the others without being readily noticed. The first indication of promotion was the award of a black peaked cap which they would take off frequently to admire and polish the shiny peak. The next step on the promotional ladder was the wearing of a black uniform buttoned high around the neck and the calves bound from knee to ankle in black puttees. For a few weeks they would strut around in our midst resplendent in this regalia then suddenly vanish, to be replaced by newcomers with armbands. In their turn they would 'don the cloth' and as suddenly disappear.

The obvious reluctance on the part of the British and Americans to work was a matter of some concern to the authorities and perhaps the finest compliment they paid to our loafing abilities was the formation of a special body of snoopers to supervise our activities. They were immediately dubbed the Gestapo by us, a name that even the Jap interpreters adopted in time. Members of the Gestapo were essentially young and nimble who could be at the top of the dock spying out the idlers one moment and be among them at the bottom the next. A favourite hunting ground for them were the so-called lavatories where there would always be a crowd of men ostensibly waiting their turn. In reality only a few of them were genuine responders to the calls of nature. Among them would be newshounds exchanging rumours, others carrying out black market transactions and the rest who considered it better to endure the stench than to work.

On the ships there would be groups of English prisoners in the compartments where riveter's fires created a cosy atmosphere. Some would sleep others smoke whilst others would be attempting to get the latest news from friendly Nips using a piece of chalk and the ship's side as their means of communication. At the slightest sign of the Gestapo a lookout would shout 'Flag Eight!' and in a flash all activity would cease with some vanishing through bolt holes while the remainder busied themselves tending the fires or searching for unused rivets in the rubbish on the deck. Fortunately the Gestapo were not mechanically minded and were incapable of distinguishing between charade and the real thing.

A former guard who had been caught stealing our sugar and who had left the army turned up in the Gestapo. Called the Sugar Bandit we immediately recognised him but in fact had no trouble with him as he was too deeply involved in a swindle with a group of prisoners. The worst of the Gestapo was a loutish youth of eighteen called Eric. He was untiring in his search for loafers and he always seemed to be here there and everywhere in his enthusiasm. As long as he could catch a malingerer he was satisfied no matter what physical exertion or discomfort was involved.

One of the jobs that Sammy Jackson and I had to do was the installation of the ash ejectors from the boiler rooms. The discharge pipes for this apparatus passed through a coal bunker in which there were numerous riveter's fires. In winter we prolonged the task as the bunker was snug and warm; whereas in summer it was hot and stifling so we would complete the job in record time.

On one particularly cold afternoon we had just bolted the last piece of piping in place when the Nip with whom we worked motioned for us to sit down. I never made a practice of sitting down because I readily fell asleep. Sammy sat down and had a nap after which he woke up and went away to light a cigarette from one of the fires. In the meantime as I leant against the bulkhead and under the influence of the warmth, I slipped over the edge of consciousness and fell asleep. When I opened my eyes Eric's revolting image seemed to fill the whole of my field of vision. By grunts and gestures he made me understand that he wanted me and I had no illusions as to what for. He started punching me about the head and as I was standing on rivets, ashes and various bits of pipe, each blow caused me to stagger drunkenly and he ended up with a few kicks for good measure. The Japs, although cowards when on the receiving end, always liked to watch a prisoner being worked over and a good crowd gathered for the spectacle, including the Nips from my own gang.

Eric's period of persecution ended when he was called up to join Nippon's armed forces; at which we all wished him a happy (and speedy) ending.

On the whole working in the ships gave us ample opportunities for loafing, especially when we were under a lazy little man called Watanabe who seemed to like us. For days we sat in the dark in the furnace spaces of the boilers, making ourselves comfortable with beds of straw. Sometimes we were able to sleep while Watanabe kept a lookout for the naval guards who dashed around like terriers seeking idlers and punishing them on the spot. Johnny, who was an inveterate smoker preferred Watanabe to any other Jap in our party because he was generous with his cigarettes. When Watanabe gave me one I would take a token puff and later give it to Johnny or one of my chums.

With our flimsy footwear it was hazardous walking about the decks of these ship cluttered as they were with air hoses, electric cables, oxygen and acetylene pipes, water hoses, as well as cinders from riveters braziers and discarded rivets, all of which could twist an ankle. There was also the deafening clatter of the riveters and caulkers, the hiss of escaping air, the splutter of the electric welders and the blast of whistles as the bosses tried to attract the attentions of the men. Working down below one was in constant danger from the gas cutters and their molten metal and from nuts and bolts discarded or thrown by the platers. We walked about crouched over to make as small a target as possible for the continual hail of missiles from the workers aloft. We stuffed straw inside our caps for protection but there was little one could do about the molten metal.

At long last the promised winter clothing arrived which consisted of discarded army uniforms with a shirt and a pair of long pants thrown in. But consistent with the Jap mentality we were warned not to wear it at work; why, we were not told. One day we returned to the camp soaked to the skin and Major Horrigan seeing our pathetic condition approached the Japanese requesting dry clothes for us. He was granted the magnificent concession to allow us to wear our greatcoats under our working clothes at work, but we must take care the naval guards did not spot them or we would be punished!

About this time the commandant had the electric light bulbs reduced in number and power. and one evening we returned from work to find that our lights were screened with lampshades, decorated incidentally with designs of bombers, searchlights and falling bombs. This of course raised our hopes that there was some allied action in this part of the world.

It may be that Ted and his friends were right. This could have been a late reaction to the Doolittle raid on 18th April 1942, when sixteen B25 Mitchell bombers, carried thither by USS Hornet bombed Japan. Led by Lt. Colonel James H. Doolittle, a reservist of the USAAF, thirteen of them bombed Tokyo while the other three dropped incendiaries on Nagoya, Osaka and Kobe. The raids themselves did little actual damage but were a boost to flagging American morale and a distinct loss of face to the Japanese. With their usual flair (as noticed by Ted) for taking it out of anyone conveniently at hand, the Japanese killed 250,000 Chinese in reprisal for helping the Americans. (See Pacific Campaign, Dan Van der Vat.)

CHAPTER 5

Nomi ka?

The end of 1942 saw our first Christmas in captivity but there was no chance of loafing at work on 24 December, the magic Christmas Eve of childhood days. The hancho, that is, the real boss of our party above Sokato, took the salute from the Dutchman in charge and with a grunt and an imperious wave sent us about our tasks. He was even more ape-like than his fellow Japs and his prominent front teeth were encased in silver. Strutting around from boiler room to engine room he hounded everyone in the party and drove us all day from 7.30 in the morning until five o'clock that night.

In the camp that night there was a special treat for the occasion. We were given the reboiled burned rice from the previous few days cooking. It was a usual practice [apart from burning the rice] to give it to us twice a week but the Christmas Eve portion was a special bonus. As a further concession we were allowed to sing carols by the wash place. We sang 'God Rest Ye Merry, Gentlemen' and 'While Shepherds Watched Their Flocks By Night'. The Dutch sang 'Silent Night' which they did wonderfully; whilst another one of theirs sounded just like 'There's No Place Like Home' Even the most hardened of us were deeply touched by this impromptu carol service and it seemed that those who professed no great beliefs in ordinary life could turn to religion for comfort in these times of stress.

To our relief Christmas day was not cold but dull with watery skies, not unlike a winter's day at home. There was no let up at work and Johnny and I with our particular working party were driven like slaves putting main steam pipes in position and bolting them together. As we worked it occurred to me that it was a marvellous opportunity to do some useful sabotage. 'Sure, it's a great idea, Ted.' Johnny said when I suggested it. So whenever we were not being observed we put nuts, bolts or any bits of metal we could find in the pipes before connecting them.

Our overseer was in a vile mood that day. Called Black Mask because he wore a black triangular mask when he had a cold, he started kicking me repeatedly as I was perched on a crazy staging high over the boiler. I dropped everything and clung with both hands to the supporting ropes and signed to him that I would rather be beaten by the naval guard than be forced off the stage. After he had finished with me he caused one of the young Nips to be severely injured. Seizing one end of a cumbersome steam pipe swinging awkwardly in the lifting tackle, he jerked it so violently that the free end swung round and swept the boy off the top of the boiler on to the floor of the boiler with the heavy pipe falling on top of him. The accident had no effect on Black Mask who continued in the same vein all day as if nothing had happened.

The hancho told our Dutch leader that work was to finish at four o'clock that day and when the time came we duly mustered to go through the counting ordeal. But when the naval guard came to find out why we had stopped they flew into a rage and sent us back to work. Meanwhile the people in camp anticipating our early return, dished out the food just before four; but as we did not return until after six our evening rice was cold and congealed by the time we ate it. However instead of the usual hot [fishy] water we were given ersatz coffee which to our amazement was sweetened. There was also an apple each—a gift from the army. When everyone in our hut had been given their apple there were six left over and in the draw for them I won an extra half.

The Roman Catholics had a service at 4.30 and we had ours after supper with a Japanese clergyman officiating. His sermon was based on 'God is with us', us obviously being the Japanese; but his English was so execrable that it was difficult to understand him although in the few phrases that I caught he called us miserable creatures and stated that the war had been forced on Japan. But apart from the sermon I quite enjoyed the service as the carols were excellent and the singing acted as a sort of safety valve to relieve our feelings.

It seems that the Japs could unbend sometimes because the army guards made an effigy of Father Christmas which they stood just inside the main gate. Finally, as a special treat I cleaned my teeth with real toothpaste (obtained on the black market with cigarettes) which I normally reserved for every third day and also washed with a piece of soap I had found in the wash place. Christmas day had been different and I turned in that night aware of a battle between my stomach and the burnt rice.

The next day we were back at work, Christmas already a memory. Johnny and I had the unpleasant task of floating the safety valves on the ship's boilers. We had to stand on top of the boilers which were fired up and with the heat coming up through our flimsy shoes and the hot air from the furnaces we were soon soaked in sweat. Fortunately before we left camp that morning I had found a piece of cloth that I had put in my pocket and as we left the boiler room I was able to strip and dry the sweat off before the long wait in the cold while we were counted.

With the aid of a piece of chalk and a few gestures it was possible to carry on quite a conversation with friendly Nips in their more expansive moods. In this way I gathered that in common with racehorses, on the first of January each year every Nip became a year older; a sort of universal birthday. The first four days of the New Year was a big holiday. Certainly 31st December had a distinct eve of holiday atmosphere with the Nips doing no work but watching us and giving us the occasional butt ends of their cigarettes. I gave mine to a pipe smoking friend, who was also a Johnson like my partner in work. As we left the yard we saw that all the buildings were decorated with sprigs of evergreen interspersed with oranges. It was a mouth-watering sight for us.

To our amazement the Nips gave us a rest while they celebrated. We could scarcely believe our luck with the prospect of four days lying on until nine o'clock each morning. Food unfortunately was scarce during that time and an Indonesian caught stealing vegetables from a store was savagely beaten and tied up near the store with a radish in his mouth.

On 1 January the Japanese soldiers began their celebrations early in the morning. They were soon violently drunk and just before noon fighting broke out among them. We remained discreetly in our rooms as, knowing what they could do to prisoners when sober, we had no desire to experience the attentions of a drunken son of Nippon. One of them less violent than his friends wandered into our room. He could speak a little English and he attacked the Japanese regime and the German army and as he was passing a few uncomplimentary remarks about the camp commandant two of his comrades burst into the room and took him away. We learnt later that he had to spend a few days in the cells for his indiscreet fraternisation with prisoners.

When not actually sleeping we passed the time playing Ludo on home-made boards. In the heat of the game it was almost as if we were on board ship again but a glance at the gaunt unshaven faces and unkempt hair dispelled the illusion.

During the holiday the temperature dropped and snow fell, blanketing the neighbouring hills. The cold struck us like a blow and our rubber and cloth boots were useless as protection, the snow melting on the cloth uppers and the water seeping through to our feet.

To celebrate our return to work—and their hangovers—the navy made us stand in the square for over half an hour in the driving snow. Many of our men were suffering from stomach problems and when they asked the guards to go behind some balks of timber nearby, they were told to do it where they stood.

Hunger, the bitter cold and repeated drenchings were causes of an outbreak of pneumonia that swept through our ranks. Dysentery was also rife and as our resistance diminished there were always new wooden boxes lined up in the passages when we came back from work; on bad days there could be as many as six.

A chief petty officer in the same work party as me was the first to get pneumonia then followed my shipboard watch-keeping chief, a friend, confidante and constant companion for over two years. With the terrible conditions undermining his will to live he quickly went into a decline. At first he recognised me when I visited him in the sick room where bad cases of illness were now sent, but after a while he looked at me with a vacant expression as if I were a stranger. Without any drugs available it was no good fetching the doctor over to see what he could do, so I used to lie beside him trying to keep him warm so that he could get some sleep. He died quietly, troubling no one but bringing to me a great sense of loss. That evening his was one of three boxes borne in a procession past our room on their way to Nagasaki.

The boiler shop was the flattering name we gave to the shack which had no sides and a very flimsy roof where we sometimes worked when we were not on the ships. While working on the boilers we had to stand on the curved top and when it got wet and greasy it was highly dangerous; even more so when there were half a dozen of us working together. To slip and fall from the boiler meant a drop of about twenty feet on to a carpet of bricks, boiler tubes and plates.

It was impossible to sit so we had to stoop or squat in Japanese style in order to use the pneumatic grinder, whilst from below us the boiler shop forges gave off dense clouds of sulphurous yellow and black smoke which swirled around us, with the sleet and snow which was driven across the open shed by the wind. The cold quickly penetrated our clothes and shoes and when water came through the air hoses, which it often did, it froze on to our hands and we lost all feeling in them. Even the Nips felt the cold and they would light fires in buckets, placing them on top of the boiler thus reducing the available space even more.

Our task was to face the pads [*grind the surfaces*] for the various valves to be connected. When the pads were faced to the Nips's satisfaction, the boiler was hoisted by a floating crane which was then towed along the jetty to the ship where the boiler was lowered and secured into the boiler room. We were then shown with great solemnity on the part of the Nips how to bolt the various valves in position and connect them to their appropriate steam pipes.' [*A job that Ted and his colleagues could probably do in their sleep.*]

Water tests on the boilers were a joy to watch as streams of water issued from various points around the furnace, boiler tubes and even the rivets. The unfortunate caulker who had to stop the leaks got thoroughly drenched while the boss men, distinguished by their smart white suits, straw hats and black puttees, looked on quite impassively. Such workmanship would have been condemned without hesitation in any other dockyard but they allowed it to pass without showing the slightest facial expression. What they said, if anything, to their workmen nobody knew.

Some of the engineers who were appointed to these ships could speak English and one of them, a Second, tried his out on me. In the course of conversation I said (tongue in cheek) that he must have been proud to be given such a fine ship with three boilers and a powerful set of engines; but he didn't rhapsodise over his fortune. He knew as well as I what a poor imitation of a ship it was and the constant fight it would be, working all hours to keep it afloat.

The ships wouldn't last long at sea. It would only need a shock like a near miss and the boilers, designed to steam at about 200 pounds per square inch and every one caulked and recaulked until they were tight, would leak like sieves. The ships themselves with their faulty rivetting would probably do the same.

Early in the year we received regular inoculations in the chest although we were not told why. There was a great deal of speculation among the prisoners.

'They're using us as guinea pigs.'

'The buggers are trying to sterilise us!'

After the first injections we were allowed a day off to recover from the effects of the jabs but the dockyard people objected and a row developed between them and the army. The dockyard prevailed however and there were no more free days.

If the inoculations were intended to improve our health they failed dismally as our men continued to fall sick; the Dutch and the

Indonesians suffering more than the British. Even though winter changed imperceptibly to the pale gold of early spring, the pneumonia epidemic continued and swept through the camp. Whilst young men who would normally have been in their prime lay dying on bare boards without even a pillow, treatment was minimal. Perhaps the Japs did not have the necessary drugs; or if they did their attitude was callous in the extreme.

When our doctor considered a man unfit for work he made out a chit to that effect which then had to be vetted by the senior medical officer, a Dutchman. If he considered it a valid case the patient was sent to the Jap doctor. The latter examined sick men three or four times a week according to his mood.

The prospective patient appeared before the doctor, chit in hand and bowed. Then followed a brief examination and a flood of Japanese which nobody could answer because they could not understand. If a man could walk a stroke of the doctor's pen through the chit and another outburst denoted that the man was fit for work.

The first time I visited the Jap quack I was suffering from acute enteralgia induced by eating the sour rice which had become our daily ration. The previous night and in the morning I had been a regular visitor to the lavatory and my stomach was sore from retching. I felt distinctly sorry for myself as I stood in front of this little man in a long white coat with jack boots underneath. He must have verified Dr. Syred's diagnosis because I was given a week in camp.

So for seven days I lazed around in the deafening silence and general idleness around me but on the first day back at work it was bitterly cold and I was feeling the symptoms of incipient dysentery. I was made to carry a heavy gas cylinder with a shipmate but was too weak to lift my end and I collapsed.

A pleasant interlude made me forget my troubles for a while when we were given four small bread rolls for our meal with a few pieces of boiled potato which were a great joy to eat.

While Ted delighted in eating his potato instead of rice in Japan, in contrast Lieutenant Kuroki Toshiro with the Japanese Army in New Guinea wrote: 'Since our arrival on 11 November we have had hardly any rice......in the front line we have to contend with a rotten supply situation and live a dog's life on potatoes,'

Then news came that Red Cross parcels had arrived in the camp. We all fondly imagined we were to get one each but the Japs doled out a parcel and a half to each room to be shared among fifty-six men.

We drew lots for our portions and my share was two and a half ounces of apple pudding. Bulk stores like sugar, salt, dried fruit and cocoa were issued and we tried sugar or salt on our bread and cocoa on the rice which made things more palatable.

The Dutchmen who had lived in such a grand way in Macassar and had asked quizzically why the English were always hungry, now made regular pilgrimages around the whole camp from room to room collecting fish bones and fish heads which they sucked avidly. A Dutch barrister was particularly fond of this practice.

From time to time the Japanese gave us questionnaires to fill in with such questions as:

> Whom do you worship or admire?
> What were your thoughts when going into action?
> Give descriptions of any deeds of heroism you saw.
> What do you think of air raids?
> What do you think of your government's policies?

Those of us who enjoyed writing really let ourselves go and imagination ran riot .

On some of our rest days we were subjected to all sorts of tests by white-coated Nips. They measured our heads and arms, noted the colour of our hair, recorded details of our teeth and heartbeat before and after exercise. All this detail was written down on forms printed in German. We also had to trace our ancestry back as far as possible with special emphasis on nationality. Answers varied from one which said, 'I don't know nothing about this' to some that needed several pages, which must have caused considerable bewilderment to the readers.

'<u>Feb. 20th to March 5th 1943</u>. Struck down with pneumonia on Sunday morning. Couldn't understand why the cutting pain in my chest would not subside, every breath was agonising. The whole day was a nightmare of pain and lightheadedness. I could feel myself suspended in space and drifting aimlessly, occasionally returning to listen to the meaningless hum of conversation of my room mates. On the following day I was moved to the sick room (often referred to as the 'death room'). As I left our room I faintly heard someone say, "Poor old Ted. Good luck, mate!"

'The words seem to burn in my brain and before I lapsed into unconsciousness I swore I wouldn't die, I had so much to live for, I wouldn't relinquish my resolve and I would fight with all my resources.'

The beds in the sick bay consisted of bare boards but the place was comparatively warm and there was the added convenience of bedpans which meant no trips to the outside toilets. A shipmate, Jock Johnston faithfully brought my meals to me each day; although for seven days so he told me afterwards, I ate nothing. I learnt later that he also brought me his own fish, potato or any other delicacy to try and make me eat. In my waking moments I remember swallowing tablets, which I later learnt were M and Bs [sulphonamide tablets made by May and Baker] These enabled me to sleep but all the time I had to take shallow breaths as, to breathe normally meant that I was wracked with excruciating chest pains. During short periods of consciousness I kept looking at the planking of the ceiling, the grain of which in one piece assumed the shape of a pair of legs. No matter where I looked my eyes were always drawn back to these legs. All the while I was delirious and in my semi-conscious state I experienced a bewildering sensation of floating in space. Sometimes I seemed to desert my body and I could see myself lying on my bed of planks.

As time passed I became more aware of my surroundings and the days of delirium faded. I was finally restored to my normal frame of mind when a young R.A.F. man two spaces from me [*on the sleeping platform*] shook the whole structure for a couple of hours, thrashing about in agony before he died. His was a tragic end and it was pitiful to see him. Before he died he was quite irrational and unpredictable; for example, when his friends offered him a drink he would try to balance the cup on his head.

The doctor in charge was a Dutchman called Weissviess, who we called Riceface as being the nearest to the Dutch pronunciation we could get. Riceface stood by and callously watched the R.A.F. boy die, making no effort to help or comfort the lad. He had so ingratiated himself with the Japs that he was never in need of food or cigarettes. He enjoyed many perquisites which he unashamedly paraded in front of his starving patients at meal times. His daily rice ration was augmented with jars of whalemeat, chili pepper and a kind of butter, whilst the sick were barely kept alive on their diet. We placed him in the same category as Quisling [*the Norwegian turncoat*] and he was aware of our dislike, to which he responded by treating us with a haughty contempt. One of Riceface's friends who passed as his secretary, used to take bread rolls from helpless patients and keep them in a locked box of which only he had the key. This delightful character was called the Bun Bandit.

While I was still in the sick room towards the end of my stay a stretcher party was sent to the dockyard and they returned with another victim of Nippon negligence. One of our lads had fallen from an insecure staging into the hold of a ship. Within ten minutes of being admitted to the camp he had died of severe head injuries.

After a fortnight I was considered fit enough to leave the sick bay but I was woefully weak and still suffering from sharp pains in my chest. I congratulated myself on either having had a light attack of the disease or else having a strong constitution; but whichever it was I was alive and determined to stay so. I was also lucky when, with a chit which said 'Pneumonia, right base'and a great deal of apprehension, I went before the Jap doctor. He had already sent a man back to work in absolutely vile weather who was only five days up from his bed of pneumonia. However all he did was to confine me to camp.

When the others had left for work the sick men who were left behind had to wash 112 bowls and 56 cups and sweep the floor, after which it was customary to curl up in the blankets to keep warm and try to forget the everlasting hunger pains. With everyone at work it was very quiet in the camp during the day and surprisingly lonely but the appearance of a few books gave us great pleasure. I read 'All This And Heaven Too' and 'Teach Yourself Spanish'. On yasumés (rest days) the feeling of loneliness was dispelled and it was like a family reunion.

During my convalescence which lasted about five weeks, three American doctors and three orderlies arrived to assist our own medical staff, which in addition to Riceface consisted of our own Dr. Syred and a tall thin Dutch doctor called Niewenhuis who we dubbed the White Buddha. The new arrivals had just come from the camp where our captain and senior officers where interned. They told us that they had been allowed to write home and had also received letters and parcels. This bit of news cheered us up considerably because we thought it might also apply to us soon.

They also told us about our [*Exeter*'s] action in the Java sea and the fate of the *Houston* and *Perth*. Both were torpedoed in the Sunda Straits. The *Perth* with her remaining torpedoes had sunk five transports. *Houston* had lost two thirds of her crew and the remainder who managed to reach the shore were murdered by the natives. This was sad news to us as the *Houston* had saved us in the first action which, we were also told, broke up an invasion force bound for Australia.

The senior medical officer of the team (Doctor Moo) wrote a report on conditions in our camp and his findings read: 'This is the worst camp I have seen for sanitation, overcrowding, poor washing facilities and long working hours.'

After this report there was a spate of promises from the Japs and we were considerably cheered with the thought of better conditions to come. But time passed and our hopes faded as we realised that as usual Jap promises meant nothing.

The month of March always seemed to be when things happened for the *Exeter*'s ship's company. On March 10 the ship had recommissioned in Plymouth after her encounter with *Graf Spee*. On the same day a year later her survivors entered Macassar camp as prisoners of war and now on March 10 1943 the remaining survivors were allowed to write home for the first time.

One of our room mates, an Australian called Bluey, was the proud possessor of a pair of hair clippers with which he kept our beards and moustaches under control. Also in our room was another who had a table knife which he whetted on a piece of stone and used as a razor. Ever since our arrival in Japan I had endured the agony of being shaved with the knife but one day, seeking a change in routine I decided to try out the clippers. Of the two forms of torture it was difficult to decide which was worse. When I was shaved with the knife it felt like a rough filing sensation which afterwards left the skin raw and sore for many days. When being cleaned up with the clippers I could feel individual hairs being pulled out by the roots. But the ensuing discomfort didn't last as long so I decided to change to Bluey and his clippers.

Our beards were a great source of amusement for us. Some were truly magnificent growths while others defied description. One young seaman trying to grow his set [*beards were called sets in the RN*] found his efforts weren't well rewarded. His beard looked for all the world like a frayed bit of linoleum stuck on his face. My own beard I thought quite good being a fine dark brown colour but the moustache was very peculiar. It was a violent colour growing out stiffly for an inch before curling back into my mouth. At the corners of my mouth there were two circles where hair refused to grow.

The weather proved to be unpredictable; one day the heat would be almost tropical and the next, cold, blustery March winds would reduce the temperature almost to freezing point. Sometimes the heavens would open all day and we would return from the yard cold and drenched. With all the doors and windows closed against the cold and sodden garments hanging everywhere, the room became as hot and steamy as a wash house.

One day we were issued with a pair of white heel-less socks and half a handkerchief each which made us wonder if the Nips were poking fun at us. The socks were far too small for any of us and we puzzled about the function of the half handkerchief. A further issue was a huge straw hat fully two feet in diameter and a straw mat which could be tied over the shoulders which the Japs gave us not so much as a protection against the rain but to bring us down to the level of coolies. On rainy days when the guards made us assemble in our straw hats and rain mats they grinned all over their faces, regarding it as a huge joke.

During the early days of April the Nips panicked over the blackout. All the lamps were removed from the passages save two, blankets were nailed across the windows and we were warned to observe a strict blackout. The blankets were not supplied by the Nips but were taken from the prisoners so we decided to draw lots to see who would lose his blankets. For once I thought myself fortunate not to draw a winning number.

My good fortune over not losing a blanket was counterbalanced when I was informed that the Jap quack wished to see me, which meant of course that I would be sent back to work. It was humiliating enough just to stand in front of him and bow but when he waved me away with an imperious gesture I was furious. He would not listen to appeals and his word was law. If you could walk you were fit for work which in a number of cases meant death. So once again I was forced to join the ranks of reluctant workers on Nippon's behalf.

Returning to work after my weeks of convalescence was terrible. The filth, noise and ever-present danger made me long for the safety and silence of the camp. The misery of this bleak existence came home to me as we were ordered about by everyone to perform the most menial tasks; beaten both by the navy [kaiguns] at work and the army guards in the camp.

My first job back in the yard was to chip a cast iron fitting. My Nip co-worker gave me a one pound hammer and a very blunt chisel while he used a two pound hammer with a good chisel. He was furious when he discovered that I had done a mere fraction of what he had and threatened me with the kaiguns and all that implied with beatings. I felt so weak that I fled in despair to the American doctor in his little hut in the yard and appealed to him for light duty. Fortunately he was on good terms with a friendly interpreter who wrote a note which was a passport for light work. For several days I passed the time making spanners and polishing rusty ones with a file.

If the days at work were grim, the nights in camp were not a great deal better due to vermin. Body lice had multiplied enormously and no matter how often our clothes were deloused we couldn't get rid of them. When I had been off work we had deloused one of our number who had a broken arm in plaster. By easing the plaster we caught 200 lice but when the plaster was finally removed the space between was found to be crawling with them and his arm eaten raw. It was remarkable how he had remained so cheerful and uncomplaining during his ordeal.

Stevo [*a Royal Marine called Stevenson*] was the first to notice the onset of body lice. He slept on the same level as me but at the opposite end of the bench. Gradually they crept along the row, until one night I caught a dozen in my clothes, making me feel miserable and unclean.

To combat them we went to 'debugging stations' every night just before turning in. After shirt and underpants had been thoroughly investigated, seeking both lice and eggs (laid in the seams) our thumbnails would be crimson where we had squashed them. Sometimes when squeezed they would squirt their contents into one's eyes, as if in a last defiant gesture. Killing as many as possible like this would give us a little respite from their attentions but they would be back in about two or three hours and I would feel them crawling around my body. Once established they were always with us; winter being the time when they were most numerous. During the day they were maddening because we wore our greatcoats and uniforms under our work suits and were unable to scratch. I noticed that if I stood by a fire there was a general movement of lice under my shirt towards the warmth.

Debugging surreptitiously took place during a curious rigmarole that the Japs introduced of massaging. At evening and morning musters every man was compelled to strip to the waist and rub himself briskly with a towel; an action during which the Japs, with unusual concern, exhorted us to avoid rubbing the nipples. We were made to do this even in the winter with inches of snow. We thought at first this was something cooked up by the Nips for us but it seemed that massaging was all part of a Jap's normal life. In proof of this were the small brushes attached to a length of string which were supplied after a while. The labels on the brushes depicted a Nip standing in his bath tub around which stood his wife and numerous diminutive progeny, all completely naked. Instead of massaging we deloused our clothes, while the room chief stood at the door to warn us of approaching Nips. At the first sign of danger we immediately began scrubbing away with our little brushes, the sound of the bristles on flesh being quite audible. Occasionally we would be caught by a guard appearing from nowhere and as punishment we would be made to stand at attention in the cold. Sometimes the unfortunate room chief got a beating on behalf of us all.

Fleas were another menace that appeared in the warmer months. After their attentions during the night we would be dappled from head to toe with red spots when we stripped for the morning massage. At the height of the season they could be seen hopping on the floor and to walk in bare feet was enough to daunt even the hardiest of us.

Nightly before retiring we would take our blankets outside to the wash place and examine them minutely, otherwise it would have been impossible to get a fairly good night's rest. They were very active and difficult to catch; the only easy ones being those surprised in their operations or those entangled in the fluffy parts of the blankets. After clearing the blankets it was then necessary to thoroughly search our clothing. Only in going through this routine nightly were we assured of at least a few hours sleep. If I caught fewer than fifty fleas from three blankets I would think that they had deserted me.

The Nips once gave us a sweet smelling powder to sprinkle on our beds and that night we all slept like logs. The next day when we searched our blankets the fleas were either dead or very groggy. We thought that this would be the end of our troubles but the powder issue was never repeated. We tried to buy it but even our most experienced racketeers could not find a supplier.

On yasumés we searched our clothing and bedding several times during the day in an effort to reduce their numbers. They were drawn irresistibly to anything white. White blankets were more thickly populated; than brown ones. Rice bowls containing a little water placed on our bunks at night would be black with their drowned corpses by the morning. The only time we had a tin of condensed milk, an unfortunate mate of mine was robbed of his luxury. They invaded the tin through the little holes he had punched in the lid and which he hadn't sealed. In the morning a black congealed stream issued sluggishly from the hole.

At the time I thought that these were the greatest scourge to be inflicted on us but then later in the summer of 1945 came the bugs [bed bugs]. Large and small they appeared everywhere, multiplying with unbelievable rapidity and all with a ferocious appetite for blood. The fleas either vanished or paled into insignificance as the bugs took undisputed hold on the whole camp. They fouled the joints between the planks with their vile excretions. A tiny bug the size of a pin's head could could inflict as bad a bite as one six times its size, injecting an irritant that lasted for three days. It was a painful experience just to lean against the woodwork in the rooms for the least contact meant an invasion of these creatures which got under one's shirt and raised blisters all over one's body. To scratch them made them worse, the bites sometimes becoming festering sores that needed treatment in the sick bay.

The bugs varied in colour from black to red and from round to torpedo-like in shape. Some were as large as a man's little finger nail while others as small as a pin's head. They were quite tender and when squashed turned into a revolting gelatinous mass that exuded a nauseating smell. They lived in the cracks in the tables and stools where we ate and to sit at table wearing shorts was a painful experience. We overcame this by sitting on a towel with the end over-hanging the stool. By the time the bugs had got around this obstacle the meal was over. They found their way into the food and they tasted as they stank. Their numbers increased so much that we abandoned the bunks and slept on the stools in the passage outside the room. However as soon as the Japs realised what we were doing this was stopped and we had to go back to our bunks. Many of our men lost so much sleep that they kept nodding off at work sometimes falling off precarious staging.

The guards, police and Gestapo were reaping such a plentiful harvest of sleeping prisoners that it was decided that something would have to be done. At a room chief's meeting the English suggested that playing a jet of steam over the woodwork and between the planks of the walls would probably kill off all the bugs. To our surprise the Nips agreed and permission was granted to start proceedings. The steam played havoc with the bugs and after our room was done we had three nights of unbroken sleep although the smell of cooked bugs was no better than raw.

One night I was so groggy that I turned in without taking even the most elementary precautions against them. At first I was aware of an insistent nibbling around my ankles, next I felt them at the back of my neck then at my waist. Still half asleep and trying to defend myself in half a dozen places at once I pursued them into my ears squashing them with a distinct squelch up my nose, into my eyes and across my lips. With face crimson with their blood and reeking of their stink I fled from my bed.

The Japs were not immune and they shared our discomfort. It was a common sight to see them delousing their clothes in the vicinity of a fire so that the bodies could be dropped into the flames. Despite that the guards used to gloat when they saw us clearing our clothes. Keeping a safe distance from us and smiling indulgently they would ask, 'Nomi, ka?' (Fleas?) as if they weren't as vermin ridden as us.

The next disease to strike our little island was spinal meningitis which was severe enough for the Jap quack to order us to gargle with Condy's Fluid when leaving the camp in the mornings and on our return at night. When the Condy's Fluid ran out warm sea water was substituted or sometimes just fresh water. As a preventive, water would hardly help and eventually gargling became a mere perfunctory gesture which we avoided whenever possible although those who were caught bypassing the process were dealt with very severely.

When a case of leprosy was diagnosed in the Indonesian quarter there was quite a panic throughout the camp. With a leper in their midst 1,500 men were under the impression that they were all now condemned to a slow and lingering death. Even when Doctor Syred told us that there was no danger of us contracting the disease many would not believe him and there was a general atmosphere of unease.

The victim was a fine athletic type of young man called Jan. He was moved to a little hut which had been hurriedly built on some reclaimed land within the confines of the camp. The only person with whom he was able to speak was the sick bay orderly who put his food three times daily at the door of his hut. To try and brighten his days of isolation we made periodic collections of books, cookies, and cigarettes for him.

From a length of bamboo, which was one of the gifts, he made a flute and which he played well. One of his favourite selections was from 'Firefly' and at night, when the wind was blowing from the sea his music wafted over to us.

He was at the window to watch us leaving for work each morning and was there again when we returned at night. He was always smiling and we would give him an encouraging wave and a surreptitious V sign as we went about our work.

One day as we went to work the familiar smiling face framed by the window was missing. This was not necessarily unusual for, on the occasions we did not see him we knew he was enjoying a 'lie in'.

But when we returned at night and saw the still vacant window we knew that something must be wrong and on asking one of the medical orderlies we were told that Jan had been taken away the previous night to a leper colony.

Time imperceptibly trickled through its hour glass until our second Christmas as prisoners of war arrived.

'Big Eats tonight boys! The Nips have opened their hearts at last!'

These words greeted us on our return from work on Christmas Eve as did the unaccustomed smell of cooked food from the galley. The authorities had issued some flour, corned beef and tins of meat and vegetables from our Red Cross supplies and the officers had been busy making 'doughboys' [*dumplings*] from these ingredients.

We each received two doughboys about the size of a small apple and they were delicious; the first real food we had had for well over a year. It was completely satisfying but the sudden intake of fat made many of us violently ill during the night although we recovered in time for the next day.

Breakfast on Christmas day included two slices of sweet potato in addition to the rice and cabbage, which seemed a promise of better things to come,

Permission was given to hold a church service in the morning which was well attended by even some of our more hard-bitten members. The singing of the carols moved us intensely and the final hymn, 'Eternal Father Strong to Save', the sailor's very own plea for Divine protection caused the familiar pricking at the back of my eyes, while some were openly crying.

At dinner time we had three buns containing sweetened beans and a fine stew after which we slept in our beds most of the afternoon to escape reality and also to keep warm. After supper we had an impromptu concert in which we all had to give a turn.

The shipyard people had sent us two packets of cigarettes and eight tangerines each which we thought was a wonderful gift (although we had to pay for them later). But it was a joy to see the smoker's enjoyment and with the doors and windows closed during our concert the temperature of the room rose until it was very cosy if somewhat foggy. When we went to bed that night we were almost happy. The Nips had been generous to us—with our own stores—and the cooks had excelled themselves. Next day we all suffered from stomach upsets but it had all been worthwhile and our feeling of well-being was sustained by the news that our names and other particulars had been sent to Tokyo for mail purposes. The weather had also been kind to us and on several occasions I was able to take off my coat when I washed which I had not been able to do the year before.

Two things were to counteract our feelings of well-being; the first was that Johnny had to leave our work party and I was left on my own to bear the brunt of Japanese behaviour. The second quickly followed. For some time 'Slinger' Woods, one of our room mates, had been lying in bed ill. He was covered in sores and infested with vermin and seemed to have lost the will to live. We had all tried to rouse him but he didn't respond and we could see him gradually drifting away from us. One morning after the hated bugle had wakened us a guard burst into our room and seeing the inert form of Slinger in his sleeping space, started hitting him. With one accord we all closed in on him,

'Leave him alone, you little bastard!'

Noting the intent in our eyes and the threat in our voices the guard ran off out of the room and we turned to Slinger to see he was all right. But he hadn't felt the guard's rifle butt because he had died in the night and the peaceful expression on his face showed that he was now freed of the existence he had found so unbearable.

In January 1944 there was a general reorganisation in the yard to increase efficiency and production. Boiler construction which had held up the output of ships was stepped up and after a while reached such a peak that there was a surplus. The big dock that the Japs had been blasting out when we first arrived was complete and there was going to be an impressive opening ceremony, although it was already in operation. Designed to be used as either one big dock or two small ones with a concrete caisson to separate the sections, two ships were being built in each section. The pair in the section nearest the dock gate were all but complete and ready for fitting out so it was decided to flood the dock and move them out to the jetty.

On that morning Sam and I were employed moving castings to the fitting out jetty and we were staggering along under a heavy load alongside the dock when, with a roar the dock gates burst open and a huge wall of water hit the two ships. As we dropped our load and fled to safety drenched to the skin, the two ships were hurled against the dividing caisson which collapsed. With a terrifying sound of rushing water and rending metal both caisson and ships smashed into the other two vessels. When the turmoil had finished there was a scene of utter devastation. All four ships were badly damaged, two of them more or less beyond recognition as ships.

There was a terrible panic. Numbers of Japs were struggling in the water and several of our men [*the prisoners*] dived in to help them, bringing most of them safely to the dock side. The situation was bizarre enough with prisoners rescuing Nips who would have done nothing had the roles been reversed; but the instant reaction of the authorities was even more astounding. The officers from both the army and the navy, plus some visiting ones, all joined forces to flog the hanchos (headmen) of the parties that had been employed on the ships at the time and who had had nothing to do with the construction or operation of the dock. Twenty Japanese workmen were killed and thirty injured in the accident while one prisoner was slightly hurt. It was discovered afterwards that not only had the gate collapsed but the sea had encroached under the floor of the dock and had burst up through it. [*Bearing out Ted's observation two years previously regarding the weak concrete mix.*]

Naturally we were all delighted at this setback but a message was transmitted on the grapevine 'Look, but don't laugh' because the Japs were very sensitive about it and to be caught near the dock with so much as a smile on one's face meant a beating.

To make up for this loss of time and production the Nips had their working hours increased. Those who came daily from Nagasaki were forced to sleep in the yard as their long working hours made it impossible for them to go home and return in time for the next day. For their extra work they were issued with soap, matches and cigarettes. Sometimes they were presented with a yard of towelling; each of them grinning with delight at this extraordinary gift. Once they were given a small bottle of chili pepper each and on New Year's Eve they were presented with a small phial of tablets to settle stomach trouble.

Shortly after the collapse of the dock, the commandant, commenting on the bravery of the prisoners who had risked their lives in trying to save drowning Nips, said that by this action America and England had proved they were A1 nations. In recognition of their bravery he presented each of them with a bottle of chili pepper.

Despite our delight at the destruction of the dock, the gas cutters worked hard to cut the wreckage into manageable proportions until the dock was once again clear. The inner section was in use again within two months but the outer section however was never used again.

Quite early in the year modifications to the ships led us to believe that the Japs were running short of vital materials. They now only fitted the ships with two boilers instead of three which reduced the power considerably. One of the newly finished ships ran aground at the entrance to the harbour because she hadn't enough power to drive against the gale and the sea running at the time.

Ted was quite correct with his conjectures. As early as January 1943 the Japanese government had introduced a plan for building wooden ships because of a desperate shortage of ship building steel and ships. Of between seventy and five hundred tons only the largest would have steel frames, so that more steel could be used for warships. By 1943 the American submarines around Japan were causing a shortage of raw materials whilst from June 1944 the American B29 Superfortresses of 20th Bomber Command were bombing all the main Japanese cities.

Despite what I had already seen I was still continually surprised by the innate cruelty of the Japanese as appallingly, they managed to surpass themselves each time. One day it was discovered that a party of Indonesians had broken into the canteen and stolen cigarettes and cookies. The Japs knew who the thieves were and as soon as they returned from work they were hauled from the ranks. They were then beaten with wooden clubs, the guards working in relays and as one Nip tired another took his place so that the continuity of the treatment was not broken. Then a further refinement was introduced. When a Nip tired he threw his victim in a judo throw across the room to another guard who took up the beating until he tired and a throw sent the victim to a fresh guard. The groans of the victims and the thud of the clubs on bodies could be heard in our room until at midnight they stopped. Next day refreshed from their night's sleep the Japs tied the thieves to stools and poured salt water down their throats.

When a Nip got angry with a prisoner he hit him, or threw at him the first thing that came to hand. A prisoner was forbidden to defend himself but often he was able to deprive the Jap of whatever he had got hold of. This of course made the Jap even more angry. An Indonesian was so goaded by a gang of Nips that he kicked over the traces and attacked them. He knocked two of them out before he was overwhelmed and beaten with iron bars that broke several of his ribs. He was tried in a civil court and sentenced to two years in gaol and we all had no doubt that was the end of him, although later on to our surprise he turned up at the camp again.

At about this time in early 1944 I felt very miserable. Accidents at work were bad. In one day one of our room mates had his head crushed in a particularly bad accident, a Dutchman was killed and another Englishman was severely injured. That night the vacant place at the table and in the ranks at muster depressed us as he was a most cheerful man who had survived numerous enemy attacks by sea and air; yet he died in the enemy's country working to help their war effort.

I also had chronic beriberi, my legs were huge, being the same size from thigh to ankle and the pain was exhausting. Doctor Syred explained to me that beriberi was a disease caused by vitamin B deficiency, but as supplies in the camp were exhausted my legs continued to swell up. Eventually my right foot swelled so much that it was three times the size of my left and painful in the extreme.

As it was almost impossible for me to walk, Doctor Syred's chit was sanctioned by the great Riceface himself and armed with this I was called to face the Jap quack. He gazed at my swollen foot for some time then through the interpreter asked if I was receiving treatment from the sick quarters. He actually exempted me from work and I came through his periodic examinations on three occasions for which I was referred to as the quack's blue-eyed boy.

[*With the sailor's fondness for nicknames all doctors were called quacks without intentional disparagement. It is noticeable however that Ted only calls the Japanese doctor 'quack'.*]

My room mates did all they could to help me and one managed to obtain some Wakamoto tablets (which contained vitamin B) from a friendly Jap who could buy them and smuggle them into the yard. He made a handsome profit on the transactions but he also took a considerable risk because business between the Nips and prisoners was strictly forbidden and offenders were severely punished. A great spirit prevailed in our camp because when my money ran out my chums provided it.

As a means of discouraging men falling ill, the Nips decided that as sick men did not work they required less food, so they decreased their rations. At dinnertime the authorities took one of the three buns from every sick man. Men under observation for tuberculosis, or lying helpless in the sick room and men blinded through accidents were all penalised. Sick men not ill enough to remain in bed were compelled to do physical training twice a day in addition to working around the camp. In this connection a situation arose with men 'sick in bed' (called shushin) and men 'sick not in bed' (cheerio). The cheerios remained in bed like the shushins and when the guards wanted some for work they could never find them. Eventually a system of tallies was evolved which were worn on the chest. The Nips could then see who was shushin, cheerio, sheiko, easo, toban or dyko; the last four being respectively: man with standing camp job, medical attendant, officer's servant, and carpenter. Thereafter the cheerios became a hounded race.

Just outside the gates of the shipyard stood a hospital, where the casualties from the yard were licked into shape to return them to work. It was surrounded by an atmosphere of filth, choking fumes and smoke. Along the road a forge belched forth clouds of thick black smoke, a little further on was a foundry adding its quota, whilst opposite the hospital was a rivet making shop which was barely visible through its own smoke. No matter from which direction the wind blew the hospital was never clear of smoke. In this atmosphere a Japanese surgeon wearing a blood-stained smock and straw soles attached to his feet by string plied his trade. His performances were quite public, through open doors and windows he was watched by a curious crowd of men, women and children. Prisoners on whom he had operated were bandaged by the stretcher party of sheikos who had brought the patient the mile and a half from the camp.

Once when the surgeon was about to operate on one of our men who had acute appendicitis, he noticed there was an air bubble in the capsule containing the anaesthetic and remarked that there was a distinct possibility of it being ineffective. As the case was urgent and there was no other anaesthetic available (it was supplied by our camp from the Red Cross stores) it was decided to continue with the operation. His concern about the anaesthetic was well-founded as it was only effective from the patient's ankles down to his feet.

One particular incident which had the whole camp fuming was the treatment of one of our seamen. On a run ashore before we were captured he caught VD and the Japs were not prepared to treat him with drugs. By the time we arrived in Japan he was suffering agonies and his penis had become so hideous that it was scarcely recognisable. The Japs then resorted to surgery and removed all outward signs of the chap's manhood. He successfully survived this outrage and did not appear to be too distressed by this primitive treatment. But when we were allowed to use the communal bath in Boy's Town it was a sad spectacle to see him in his double nakedness until we became accustomed to it.

Lack of medical supplies inspired the doctors to experiment in making up a few basic requirements. The White Buddha produced a form of Vaseline from machine grease we had filched from the yard which he used for dressing wounds. One day one of his assistants came to the bench at which I was working to scrape up iron filings to further the Buddha's research. As a result of this gleaning he produced some kind of lotion. Charcoal, used with good effect on stomach disorders was another of the Buddha's enterprises. He produced sticks of it which patients would chew, whilst the more squeamish crushed it into a powder and washed it down with water. Doctor Syred discovered that Barbasol was excellent for treating open wounds. Barbasol was an American shaving cream and he filled gaping wounds with it, using the cellophane wrappings of cigarette packets as bandages, It was wonderfully effective.

Doctor Weissviess, or Riceface was by far the most unpopular person in the camp, an arrogant overbearing man who was always antagonistic towards our Doctor Syred and for whom he had a violent dislike. He was openly hostile to the British, an attitude which pleased the Jap quack with whom Riceface, aided by Budding the interpreter, ingratiated himself. As a result of this friendship Riceface was never without food or tobacco and was one of the most influential people in the camp. Some of his diagnoses were as diabolical as those of the Jap, his chief aim being to help in sending as many sick and ailing men as he could to work. We came to the conclusion that the Nips worked a bonus system for him; the more sick people he could get to work the more luxuries he could have.

Riceface employed a primitive form of surgery while cutting out boils, carbuncles abscesses or swellings. He worked at a table in the centre of a room lined with benches on which sat the would-be patients awaiting their turn and watching the one being operated on. He would never use local anaesthetics which were readily available and each whimper from his victims drew from him a flood of Dutch invective. In full view he was seen to probe right through one man's foot and another's hand with a pair of scissors, after which he flushed the holes with Condy's Fluid. The idea of hot fomentations never entered his head, the knife being the only agent he and the Jap quack used for healing. Some of the men treated for abscesses in the hand had mere claws left when he had finished, the fingers being permanently bent and immovable. However it should be said that he was never adequately supplied with bandages and dressings. Often there were neither and the men stole rags from the yard for bandages, while small pieces of mosquito netting, supplied by the prisoners were used as swabs and dressings.

I went to him on three occasions, the first being by reason of a huge carbuncle with seven heads on the back of my neck. It had become extremely painful and the slightest movement of my head was agony. Even to blink my eyes was torture. My mates used to dress me for work and the walk to the yard was unbearable; so in desperation I went to the sick room and placed myself at his mercy. For once he didn't dispute Doctor Syred's chit and I was told to report to him the next morning.

After watching a gruesome exhibition of his technique on a dozen or so patients, I was called to his table. While placing my head in a suitable position he ground my face into the table top and my growl of protest was drowned in a flood of uncomplimentary Dutch. He proceeded without anaesthetics as usual to cut out the carbuncle and by the pain he caused, part of my neck as well. For a quarter of an hour in that unheated room I sweated copiously all the while tapping with my foot on the floor and locking my jaws to suppress the slightest sound. At last he stopped and I heard the tinkle of the instrument falling into the tray.

'Look, you can play golf!' he said, from which I concluded that the hole he had dug was big enough for a golf ball.

That night my temperature soared to 104 and at midnight the Jap quack, who was violently drunk examined me and decreed that I was fit for work. At the yard next morning I reported to Doctor Syred in his little hut in the yard and, taking my temperature which was still 104, he sent me back to camp together with ten others who were unfit. Arriving back at camp the Jap quack's assistant flew into a paroxysm of rage and made us kneel on the concrete for two hours during which time he reviled us in an attempt to provoke us. However nobody responded and I for one was too preoccupied in trying to retain consciousness to take notice of him.

My immediate problems were far from over as three boils erupted on the other side of my neck, which were removed by the butcher, though with far less pain than the carbuncle. Each day for a week Riceface spooned out the pus from the the boils with evident enjoyment finishing up each session with the tinkle of the knife into the bowl and a satisfied 'Zo!'. The worst was then over for another twenty-four hours.

One day Riceface spoke to me in French and was so surprised when I answered him in the same language that, from then on, his attitude towards me changed considerably. From that day whenever we met he spoke to me in French, confessing at one time that he thought mine was 'a terrible carbuncle'; which was about the nearest thing to sympathy I ever heard from him.

My third encounter with Riceface was with an abscess on my foot which made my toes swell enormously. For two days he probed with his knife to locate it while the pain seemed to radiate from my foot like ripples on a pool.

There were other slightly less painful ways of getting out of work. In the yard we were surrounded by electric welders and to watch the beautiful sizzling arcs without goggles could cause a severe inflammation of the eyes which made it impossible to see next morning. This condition was called a flash and was certain to gain a chit for a day off work. Then one day one of our number accidentally got some chili pepper in his eyes and the resulting inflammation was identical to that of flash. From then on—when supplies of chili pepper were available—we induced artificial flash if anyone wanted a day off; the discomfort suffered was well worth the twenty-four hours from work.

Sufferers from diarrhoea were required to bring a sample every day to Riceface to get off work and some were able to retain their chits long after they were better by getting a chum to provide the evidence. The practice was brought to an end when some informer told Riceface about it. From then on he decreed that sufferers would have to produce their own evidence before his very eyes.

At about this time the news of Tojo's resignation and the start of work on an air raid shelter had the camp buzzing with rumours.

Both events were linked to the capture of Saipan in the Mariana Islands by the Americans in July 1944. The failure of the garrison to hold the island tipped the scales of public and political opinion against Hideki Tojo, Japanese prime minister and Chief of the Army Staff, forcing him to resign on 18 July; and the use of Saipan airfields brought Kyushu and southern Honshu within easier range of American B29 Superfortresses, which had been operating from China since 14 June.

CHAPTER 6

Bo-go-go and Yo-yo Poles

'<u>Sept. 3rd [1944].</u> A very bad month for us because Dr. Syred was caught by the snooping sergeant reading the news to the patients in the sick room, the pity of it was that it was two days old. The doctor was put in cells for a while with two of the sick bay staff and we were asked on the parade ground if any of us had written the news which was on a cigarette packet. After a while we thought that the explanation given by our chaps that it was merely a collection of rumours for the benefit of the sick men was good enough. [*The Japs believed this and the doctor was freed*]

'Then followed an incident in the yard when an Indonesian was caught trading with the Japs and informed them of our news service, with the result that a Dutchman was apprehended and tortured.

'An activity that annoys both the army and the navy is the trading that takes place between us and cooperative Nips in the shipyard. Almost anything, including newspapers but with the exception of food can be had providing one has the money. The Indonesian thought he would escape punishment by betraying the news service and a Dutchman called Brandan was arrested and was so badly tortured that he fainted several times. Each time he was brought round with water and tortured again and again; but he resisted all their demands for information. He was left in an appalling condition and had to be carried back to camp. The inquisition was by no means over for the army tied him to a stake outside the guard house for several nights. Finally on the advice of Major Horrigan he gave the kaiguns all the information they required. The enterprising Nip who supplied the contraband newspapers was taken away from the yard and never seen again.'

'<u>September 15th.</u> The Dutchman in cells through the news racket is now free but has to remain in the sick room to recover from his injuries. He's certainly a stout fellow!

'For a while the news service has been suspended as the Nips are still not completely satisfied that we are in ignorance of what is going on in the outside world. In an attempt to stop any trading whether for news or goods they have collected all jewelry, rings, bracelets and watches.'

When we had first arrived in Japan, Nippon was everywhere victorious. Their successes were prodigious and against this backcloth the Nips treated us with an irritating condescension. They continually reminded us of 'Repulso', 'Prisowellso' and 'Singaporu' [*Repulse, Prince of Wales* and *Singapore*], raising their hands above their heads to indicate surrender. Little boys would lunge at us bayonet fashion with pieces of wood while older men smiled indulgently and motioned that although the little boys were small they were very strong.

On our little island we felt very isolated, our exile being further compounded by the lack of authentic news. Occasionally the officers were permitted to read an English language newspaper called '*Mainichi*' from which they passed on to us any interesting items of news. The first memorable news flash was of Stalingrad where the Germans had suffered a notable defeat [*November 1942*]. The Nips referred to this in a most lofty manner as a debacle as if the word defeat was not to be found in their language. News items like this sustained our morale and we had no doubt regarding the final outcome of the war but we still wanted to know when the Japs would be attacked.

Gradually a news service was organised—largely owing to the efforts of Brandan—and when we began to get wages for our dockyard work we decided to put ten cents a month each to pay a contact at work to bring the *Mainichi, The Nippon Times* (English language paper) and a Japanese paper into camp. A Chinese boy with a good knowledge of Japanese translated the contents of the Jap paper whilst the outstanding news from the English language papers were abstracted and a digest, written on cigarette packets, made of the whole. While this was going on the doors and windows of the hut were tightly packed with men seemingly in deep discussion acting as a screen. Official readers then visited the various rooms to read the news. It was good to lie in our bed spaces listening to the news, especially when on one occasion it read: 'the German army is in full retreat.'

For a few months the authorities actually issued us with the *Nippon Times* but as a propaganda ploy it was not a great success. At first it published items which some of us were willing to accept as partly true because at the least they indicated where the fighting was going on at that time. More often than not the news stories were unbelievable nonsense that nevertheless provided great entertainment and whether the Japanese public believed them or not, the laughter they provoked among us was a great boost to our morale. The paper went to great lengths to prove that our 'little pirate' Sir Francis Drake was an arch-villain that we should be ashamed to acknowledge as a great seaman. Our patron saint St George came in for denigration as well.

On the other hand we were told that Nippon scientists had discovered how to make flour in the tundra districts which would greatly assist the Japanese garrisons on the islands of Attu and Kiska in the Aleutians and at the same time relieve the strain on resources at home. This item confirmed a previous edition which had claimed Japanese successes in those islands, although we couldn't see why they invaded them in the first place.

Another article described how an airman, after completing a most dangerous mission came in to make his report to his commander and promptly collapsed. On examination it was found that the intrepid flyer had been dead for hours. It was his indomitable spirit that had driven his body on to make his final report thereby revealing the superior qualities of the Nippon race. We also read of an airman who brought down an American aviator with a weapon no more dangerous than a rice ball. The American thought it was a hand grenade and crashed his plane.

At sea there were other heroes. A sailor, seeing that his ship was in imminent danger of collision with another, dived overboard to use his body as a fender. Then there was the wily admiral who succeeded in luring two American fleets together and bringing them to action against each other.

[*Cunning plans from enemy admirals were generally quite unnecessary to cause ships of either side to fire on their own kind.*]

Scores of times the easy optimism of that paper was disproved by the true events and shortly after the Americans had retaken Attu and Kiska the issue of the paper was stopped; a fact which in itself we regarded as favourable news because the Germans were reported to be fighting defensive battles.

One *Nippon Times* report that worked to our detriment was about there being no leather either in Britain or the United States. Not long afterwards the Red Cross parcels included a consignment of boots which cheered us all up. But next morning when we paraded in our new boots we were told to take them off and wear the old rubber and cloth ones. Presumably after the statement in the *Nippon Times* the Japanese workmen in the yard would have been incensed to see our superior leather footwear.

The White Buddha gained our admiration and proved himself a man apart from the usual run of Dutchmen, when he openly defied the Nips. In defiance of the general order regarding the wearing of leather boots to work, he continued to wear them. When confronted by the authorities he told them that he was primarily a doctor not a prisoner of war and they had no jurisdiction over him. The Japs responded by clapping him in cells 'to learn discretion'. He was a very tall man and it was impossible for him to stand upright or lie full length on the floor. He must have had to fold himself up like a jack knife in order to sleep. When he was released he was unrepentant and continued wearing his boots, thereby setting an example which many of us followed.

One night as we were about to leave the yard we were searched by the hanchos (bosses) of our parties. This was the beginning of numerous searches, for newspapers or money to buy news, which the hanchos later delegated to schoolboys. These children almost stripped us and we even had to take off our boots. A few of them spoke English and when a prisoner opened his mouth to protest they would say: 'Do not speak!'.

On one occasion after having been searched by these monkeys we were again searched by the army on arrival back at camp. After dispersing from the parade ground, we found our rooms in complete confusion, blankets and clothes were strewn all over the place and everywhere there were reams of toilet paper. My heart sank at the thought of them discovering my diary.

But the Nips seemed only able to think of one thing at a time and this time the object of their search was money, so they concentrated on that. Among my possessions that they had thrown about were pencils and writing paper, highly forbidden articles, some cuttings from newspapers and a small map of Europe on which I used to follow the war. All these things had been overlooked and as we tidied up everyone kept bringing me sheets of my diary from around the room and I didn't lose a single page.

'December 25th 1944. "God rest ye merry, Gentlemen"; brave words under these awful conditions. Sometimes I think that those who perished in the action are really better off than us but after all life is sweet, if only we can survive this winter we shall be well on the way. A really wonderful Christmas this year, Canadian Red Cross parcel between six men. The fruit from the parcels was cooked in the galley and served for breakfast, in addition to the rice we had about two or three pounds of sweet potatoes each. It took most of us all our time to finish the meal. Dinner consisted of rice and stew plus three buns containing sweetened beans.

'A fine concert in the afternoon in the bathroom and was very much appreciated by everyone. The artistes were very fine indeed especially one made up as a gorgeous French mademoiselle. [She] was hardly ready [in time] to come on the platform and the orchestra had to play "Parlez-moi d'Amour" several times before she made her appearance.

'Thoughts, scarcely coherent and almost delirious, [of] home all the time. On the whole a wonderful day, weather really beautiful.

'I notice Bo-go-go was present at the concert with his eyes everywhere at once, presumably looking for trouble; but it seemed obvious that he was under orders not to disturb us and the restraint seemed irksome.

'In the evening we had in addition to the rice and stew a small lump of extremely hard beef. Anyway, the gesture was there and in any case not many were able to finish the meal.

'We had a sing-song to finish off the evening and so concluded another Japanese Christmas.'

When we first arrived in Fukuoka Camp the sergeants in charge of the army guards were fairly easy going and except for occasional bouts of violence (which was normal Japanese behaviour) they were almost rational human beings. But as they were replaced from time to time their successors became increasingly irrational. One who we called Chinny, because he just didn't have one, joined the camp as a corporal and must have felt his inferiority, which he took out on us. When he was duty shuban he would inspect our room at night and as we stood in our two ranks each side of the table his temper would flare up at the sight of a man an inch out of line. Taking off his leather belt he would lash out at everyone within reach with the buckle end of the belt. At the end of his inspection, bloody faces and black eyes indicated more clearly than any written notice that 'Chinny was here'. When he got his promotion he mellowed considerably and became quite bearable.

Then just before Christmas 1944 there arrived one who was a ringer for Macassar's Goldtooth and in direct contrast to his immediate predecessor, a buck-toothed individual whose only interest was in taking as much of our Red Cross food and stores home as he could.

One of this new sergeant's responsibilities was the building of an air raid shelter in the camp and as the Japanese for air raid shelter sounded something like Bo-go-go, this was the name we gave him; or Bogo for short. Each day he kept a small party back from the yard to work on his project but in order to speed it along he would prowl around the passages in the evening, picking on people for the most trivial offences like singing or laughing, having their hands in their pockets, wearing their hat on the back of their head or sometimes just looking at him. The men thus conscripted had to work for two hours on three nights in their own time.

When the shelter was finished Bogo tested it on one of our rest days. We were crammed into it, supposedly to half capacity but even then it was so stifling that the temperature rose by four degrees in a quarter of an hour. Shortly after, a night of torrential rain undermined one of the walls and the whole thing collapsed and work began on another.

One of Bogo's first acts was to revive old camp regulations which had by mutual consent fallen into disuse. One of the most annoying was to forbid us to strip off in the wash place for our nightly swill down after work. The first wash place had been outside the building and there were two long benches with built-in troughs over which ran a water pipe. During the previous winter several men had contracted pneumonia through washing in the open wash place, so it was forbidden to strip, but in the summer this rule was suspended. When Bogo came along he decided to enforce it and with the temperature up to ninety degrees, sweating filthy men were not allowed to take off their shirts to wash their sweat soaked bodies nor could they take their boots off to wash the black clinging mud from their feet. When a general howl of protest went up Bogo replied, 'Men must not catch pneumonia.'

Mass disobedience followed to which Bogo responded by ordering the guards to deal with the situation, which they did with great enthusiasm, using their rifles, bayonets and their heavy steel-shod boots. Bogo also gained a considerable bonus, for huge parties were enlisted from offenders for work on air raid shelters and gardens. (The sudden panic to cultivate gardens was due to the visit of an official who was in charge of all prisoner of war camps in Japan. He had expressed disapproval on seeing so much of the land around the camp uncultivated.)

As far as washing was concerned we decided that it was probably better to be filthy and sound of limb than clean and crippled, so Bogo got his way. Later a bath was introduced and the rooms were put on a roster for going first. The problem then was that the lower a room was on the roster the murkier the water got and to make matters worse it was salt which made one feel even dirtier.

One of my chums, a camp worker called Blacky used to smuggle a bucket of fresh water into the room for me and on arrival from the yard I would strip off and swill down in the corner of our room. I did this so often and regularly that I got very careless. One day when I was soaping down my legs I suddenly became aware of an ominous silence, just as if a clock on the wall had stopped after running continuously for years. Turning around I found Bogo standing right behind me, his face creased in a diabolical grin and a look of triumph in his eyes. Immediately a crowd gathered to watch my fate—I could never understand the mentality of people who would watch a fellow suffer.

'Nan ka, O mya?' ('What are you up to, Inferior One?')

Although I didn't know at the time what he said I knew what he meant.

'Can't you see, you stupid bastard?'

Despite the brave words my heart was hammering at the back of my throat as I snapped at him. Then another of my chums, also a camp worker who had learnt a little Japanese explained that, as my legs were covered with festering sores it wasn't hygienic to get in the bath with the other men. Quite uncharacteristically Bogo remained perfectly calm and the normal outburst failed to erupt. Instead he took my number and strutted off out of the room. For some time I lived in suspense waiting for the axe of Bogo's judgment to fall. Days swelled into weeks and weeks into months and to my relief I was never brought to book.

Bogo seemed able to exert an enormous influence over the various camp commandants that we had. Shortly after he arrived the Jap major in charge—known to us as the 'Camp Tramp' because of his scruffy appearance—left and a younger captain took his place. For a while he was quite considerate towards us; floggings were dispensed with and he promised to rectify 'injustices'. He abolished the practice of us having to salute the guards and altogether life seemed to take a turn for the better. This did not please Bogo and he kept nagging the commandant until he finally convinced him that life was too easy for us and once again the savagery started. Camp workers received no respite and Bogo's whereabouts were signalled from one end of the camp to the other just as the movements of Gold Tooth had been in Macassar. Even his own men hated him and warned the prisoners of his approach.

At one time great quantities of timber were needed for the construction of the air raid shelters which presented Bogo with a wonderful opportunity to curtail our leisure. Instead of detailing a party to bring the timber into the camp he would wait for us as we left work then march us to where the timber was stored. Each man had to take a balk of timber under the eye of a sentry who would decide if the chosen load was too light. At first we all chose the lightest pieces until the guards cottoned on, so it was found safer to choose a 'middling' balk; although some guards got great pleasure in making prisoners carry cripplingly heavy loads. After staggering back to camp we stacked the timber in orderly piles under the watchful eye of Bogo who punished anyone not placing it neatly or who inadvertently knocked a pile over.

Another chore on which we had to work well into the evening was carrying tiles to mend the hut roofs. Originally the huts were covered with wafer-thin wooden shingles about three inches square that had rotted away, with the result that in the rainy season the water poured into our rooms. Even Bogo thought this an impossible situation so it was decided to repair the roofs. The tiles were made by Koreans about a mile from the yard and after work we were marched down to the works. The first away had more time in the camp afterwards than the unfortunates bringing up the rear, so there would be a mad scramble as, with the guards and police screaming at the tops of their voices, each of us collected four heavy tiles to take back to camp.

At first we had to stack them under the watchful eye of Bogo who kicked over any piles he didn't like; but then he came up with the idea that we should deliver them to the roof on which they were needed. One could see the obvious joy in his eyes when he explained this to us. One by one a thousand men had to climb a single ladder on to the roof and place the tiles in position for the workmen, then descend by another ladder at the other end of the building. Bogo gloated over this scene for months while it lasted. No excuse was accepted from anyone if he was unfit or had no head for heights and there were several casualties through men becoming dizzy and falling from the roof. What with the final counting and recounting of our numbers to make sure no one was missing it was well past eight o'clock before some of us reached our rooms to find that our rice, which had been dished out at six o'clock, was black with flies.

Work on the roofs caused a serious accident which had the unexpected result of Doctor Syred's reputation being considerably enhanced. As a young British doctor he had been continually denigrated by Riceface. When he declared a man unfit, Riceface as senior doctor overruled his decisions and sent the man to work. At one time Riceface had managed to influence the Jap doctor into declaring Doctor Syred unfit to practice.

The accident happened when a party of our men were working on a roof and one of them came in contact with a high tension cable. Another lad rushing to his aid was severely burnt and both fell to the ground. Luckily Doctor Syred was in camp and was on the scene almost immediately closely followed by Riceface. At once the two doctors disagreed about treatment whilst the twitching bodies lay at their feet. Doctor Syred had treated many similar cases during the blitz in London and had experience that Riceface lacked. So he remained determined and stoutly resisted Riceface's suggestions, who seeing that Syred was not going to budge said he would wash his hands of the whole affair.

For a while the man was critically ill and on the brink of death. Doctor Syred however, never relaxed and so great was his determination and personality that the patient started pulling through, despite the lack of medical supplies. To clean the wounds Doctor Syred introduced maggots into them and when the dressings were removed there was healthy flesh which in time left very little scarring. The only permanent reminder of the accident was the loss of the use of one finger.

[*Doctors in America are just now (1995) rediscovering the beneficial effect of maggots in a wound, first noted in the Napoleonic Wars.*]

His care of this casualty was typical of the man whose persuasive manner overcame the fears of his patients and, in the absence of medicines and equipment, instilled in them a confidence in the natural healing powers of the human body. From our earliest days in Japan we were more than grateful to him for his continual quiet encouragement and for the way he endured the beatings when standing up to the Japs on our behalf.

The Japs always impressed me as being a spartan race and considering their size they were capable of amazing feats of strength over short periods but through their own stupidity they dissipated their energy in doing things the hardest way. They had what we termed a 'yo-yo' mentality after the yo-yo pole with which they carried everything. The load was secured to a sling through which the pole was threaded and away they would trot, the pole on their shoulders, with a sing-song chant to keep in step. One day we watched four Japs struggling to move a heavy weighing machine with two yo-yo poles, totally ignoring the fact that the machine had four wheels on which they could have pushed it along quite easily.

For us the yo-yo pole became a symbol of our slavery. Sammy and I had the job of carrying the heavy castings from the stores to the ships at the fitting out jetty with yo-yo poles. On arrival at the jetty we then had to climb two flights of steps and, in our weakened state each step caused our knees to buckle. By the time we reached the top we were exhausted but the kaigun stationed there made certain by means of his rifle butt that we didn't take a rest. Stepping from the platform on to the deck of the ship was another tricky manoeuvre as the load would slide down the pole hitting the front man forcibly in the back; something that entertained the Nips enormously until we mastered the technique. Once on board we had to scramble over a maze of air and gas pipes, water hoses, electric cables, piles of cinders and discarded rivets all of which rolled as we stepped on them. Inside our flimsy cotton and rubber footwear our feet slithered around in black slime caused by a mixture of dust and sweat. The least stumble made the load swing about which in turn made us stagger like drunks much to the amusement of the two small boys who were our minders.

Even in the very bitter winter weather most of the Japs walked around with a shaped piece of wood on their bare feet kept on by a length of plaited straw which passed between the big toe and its neighbour. A more refined type of footwear consisted of a number of small blocks nailed to a strip of canvas which had the added virtue of flexibility. But until we got used to it, the sight of an otherwise well-dressed Jap in European clothes with these odd looking sandals seemed ludicrous.

The first type of boot the Japs issued to us consisted of a rubber sole with an upper of thin black cloth. There was a separate compartment for the big toe and the boot was fastened at the back by a clip. They were as cold as ice and quite comfortless in spite of our attempts to improve matters by stuffing them with straw. In the winter the thawing snow or the rain soaked through the cloth while during the summer there was the combination of dockyard dust and sweat to contend with. In the room at night the smell from the boots was overpowering but we could not leave them outside because they would be stolen.

These boots were replaced by an inferior kind (if that were possible) with an ersatz rubber sole and an upper made from a striped material which reminded me of sun blinds. Mine had cherry and white stripes, were at least six inches too long and had to be packed. They were the most awkward things to wear, tripping us up and making us feel like clowns. Eventually this supply of footwear petered out too and we had to use our Red Cross boots, although many had worn theirs out by this time around the camp.

From the time we started wearing our real boots to work I nursed mine. On the way to and from work I always tried to walk on the bare earth rather than the sharp stones and pebbles on the road. I stole grease to preserve them and did everything I could to prolong their life. But after all my care at work I stepped on a hot rivet and burnt a neat hole in the sole of my left boot and from then on the slightest shower was enough to ensure a wet foot. I bought another pair from an American for three packets of cigarettes and five bowls of rice but they were no more watertight than the others. But from the same man I also bought a pair of underpants which I thought were dazzling with their red, green and white stripes. With their bright colours in contrast to our drab surroundings I always felt a certain boost to my morale when I wore them.

For nearly eighteen months the only protection against the torrential rain that the Japs gave us was the coolie hat and straw mat; but they did not last long for, after a few soakings, they mildewed and rotted away. In the camp there was, as we all knew a store full of raincoats but with their usual perversity the Japs refused to give them out. Then some inventive soul among us came up with an idea. The Japs used sacks made of straw which were quite thick and durable and our genius cut a hole in the bottom of the sack for the head to go through and one in each side for the arms and although our raincoats gave us an odd scarecrow appearance, we did at least keep dry.

We wore these coats for a while but then one night the Japs stopped us at the gates of the yard and in pouring rain, made us take them off while they, dressed in their waterproof hats and coats, performed their interminable counting routine. From then on the sacks were prohibited. Shortly after this to our surprise and delight we were each given a raincoat from the store. Wondering at the change of heart, in the pouring rain next morning we happily put on our coats—to be told by the Nips we could not wear them.

In time the Japs relented and we were allowed to wear them and they proved a boon; not only in keeping us dry but for smuggling contraband into the camp.

'January 1st 1945. Two days ago our fondest dream was fulfilled, a complete Red Cross parcel a man, first time in three years. The Japanese NCOs however did all in their power to prevent it, trying to dole it out in petty amounts as on previous occasions; but the word of the commandant prevailed. We were all like children, in fact worse. Wrappings were undone with trembling fingers and contents sampled. Today there was a plethora of pudding making; a sure indication of unruly stomachs in the near future.

'The guards seem in a much better mood than last year and the worst kaigun guard has been relieved, much to our relief.'

'January 14th. Since writing last there has been a terrible accident in the yard [when] one of the Indonesians had his foot severed by a falling plate. He was taken to the hospital and lay on the table some considerable time before the doctor operated. The boys who carried him in could hear his cries during the operation. I am glad to say he is making good progress in the sick room.'

The Indonesian had a sudden urgent need to go to the toilet and instead of climbing up from the bowels of the ship by the long awkward ladders, he decided to crawl out through an unplated space in the ship's side, unaware that this hole was about to be plated. The Nips custom when plating was to lower a plate into position with a crane, catch one corner of the plate and hold it with a single bolt whilst they positioned it for the riveters. A plate had been secured by one corner and just as the man put his foot through the open space, the sling snapped. The plate pivoted on the bolt and swung down like a gigantic guillotine and severed his foot just above the ankle. The men working in the bottom of the dock had a shock when a foot encased in a rubber boot fell on them in a shower of blood.

(Despite a gangrene scare he made a good recovery; but he must have felt his loss terribly because he had been a wonderful athlete.)

'January 28th. Received a letter from home containing a photo of Mum and Dad. They haven't altered in the slightest; as hale and hearty looking as ever. The little I can see of the garden and the surrounding houses make me very home-sick. The most momentous event is the disposal of our Red Cross parcels by the Nips. The day before yesterday enough parcels arrived for each man [to have one]. We all anticipated a fine yasumé but yesterday a circular letter informed us that we were allowed to have raisins, chocolate, sugar, coffee and chewing gum. The remainder, three tins of meat, the butter, milk, jam and cheese would be issued through the kitchen.

'Imagine our intense disappointment when we heard this awful news and today we have seen how our property is being disposed of. Already 80 tins of milk have been taken and sent to the galley, so we should have what the Nips see fit to leave us. It seems they are intensely jealous of everything we receive from the Red Cross. Packages of Red Cross comforts arrived with the food and the Nips had the audacity to issue this gear to the best workers in the yard. This was done this morning and those fifth columnists the Indonesians and Dutchmen and I am sorry to say some Englishmen had their choice [*of the clothes*].

'Just heard that some of the Indonesians and Dutchmen are agreeable to pooling their "prizes" they were given this morning. The officers were lectured this morning by the camp commandant that there was too much complaining and the men behave as if they were entitled to the Red Cross [*parcels*]. Also that the officers were inciting mutiny but the men should feel grateful to the Japanese because they had at great sacrifice provided shipping to bring this stuff to Japan. It looks as if things are going badly for them. Please God deliver us from these heathens!'

'February 9th. Great purge on the news these last few days. An American in the jug and his friend very badly beaten. An American in the same room gave them away to the Nips. What a disgraceful affair. This was followed by a search of the rooms, we came back from work to find all our stuff upside down. What a sickening sight!

'An awful month this, constant hail, sleet, rain and snow; temp. almost constant at 28 degrees. This has been a far worse winter than the first one here. A couple more deaths in the camp and only the coming of the fine weather is going to save many of the Aussies, the majority of whom have never seen snow before. Since the last Red Cr. we have a bowl of milk each last yasumé and 4 oz of cheese. Today we received the pickings from the 'rich Nips's table' – our raisins, soap, choc, chewing gum, coffee and sugar.

'Seems the Nips have had a bad time, the one we work with being perfectly vile this week. No wonder if the latest rumours are true: Russians 15 kilometres from Berlin and the Allies 60 miles the other side: and news of the Japs losing the Philippines. [*More or less true; give or take a few miles in Europe and weeks in the Philippines*] Despite the pin pricking treatment of our captors the morale of the camp is rising. I wonder if we shall have another disappointment, it's so awfully cruel to have one's hopes come crashing down in ruins.

'The photo of Mum and Dad is now a constant source of comfort to me, I wonder why Thyra hasn't written. I haven't heard from her for the last four or five mails.'

'February 25th. Last few days have been fine with weather just like Easter at home, hard bright days like jewels. It has been wonderful to stand up on the ship without feeling the cold. The new guards are extraordinarily mean. It is manifest that now under Bo-go-go they have had a thorough coaching. Latest pin prick; the guards insist that as we leave the lavatory we rinse our hands in two tiny wooden basins. Two for 1,500 men and rarely changed. Fancy these filthy monkeys teaching us about hygiene.

'Several men are becoming informers with a result that two men have been confined to cells without food and beaten terribly, possibly because they had something to do with the news. Now the major [Horrigan] is in cells and no-one knows why. An American is in because he has been continually stealing his messmates' food. How our morals are sinking is illustrated by an example in our room. One of the fellows bringing food from the galley stole a fish from the tray; there being only 18 fish for the 45 in the room. Another stole milk and sugar from the next bunk. It is beginning to tell on us, this confined living.'

'March 4th. February went out with a burst of glorious weather, it has been marvellous not to be conscious of the cold. The informers have been very successful, several men have been put in cells and kept there for some time. The worst treatment was given to an American. He was kept without food and water for five days and kept awake for the first 24 hours. Food was placed in front of him but not given him. Anyway he is out now and save for two black eyes just as perky as ever. The major remained some days in cells, he is now at large. The trouble seems to be the news situation and the Nips are trying to trace the source of all our rumours. Sometimes it seems that we have been here all our lives and will continue to seem so now that we have no rumours.

'Our Red Cross food is being stingily distributed in dribs and drabs; three times we have had 3 oz of tinned meat, but today they went mad and gave us a tin of corned beef between two.'

'March 18th. This last week we have had an [air raid] alarm every night and sometimes two or three in one night, but last night was the best. After the siren was sounding all night, instead of our 7 o'c rice we had to go into the air raid shelter at 6 o'c.

'The Gestapo has been granted special powers this week to beat prisoners, which they do on every possible occasion with a length of rubber tubing.

'Heard that the Indonesian who was sent to jail for defending himself against the Nips in the yard has just died. The medical major was beaten by a little sick berth orderly for breaking a syringe. He had to kneel down so that the Nip could reach him.

'The siren has just sounded again, (2 o'c.)

'All clear about 5.15. We have had nothing to eat since 9 o'c this morning. The organisation has fallen over due to the air raids.'

The first indication we had of expected air raids was when the Japanese interpreter told us in a heavy American accent that in the event of one we had to lie low and place ourselves in the hands of the army. He also told us that an anti-aircraft battery had been installed on the hill overlooking the camp just outside the gate. Then by the huts of Boys Town there appeared long shaky bamboo ladders and fire beaters consisting of bamboo poles with lengths of knotted straw attached to one end. They did not impress us greatly as fire fighting equipment but shortly after water mains were laid around Boys Town and we were more impressed when trailer pumps and stirrup pumps made their appearance. The young Nips were organised into fire parties which practised periodically, with the boys wearing hoods that enveloped their head and shoulders whilst the hanchos wore steel helmets.

The neighbouring hills were transformed into huge rabbit warrens and on our daily excursions to and from work we passed a sheer cliff into which the Nips were tunnelling. Day after day they blasted away without any outward signs of progress, the operation continuing for so long that we began to lose interest. Then one evening as we were returning to camp along the path below the cliff, we were scarcely about thirty yards from it when the whole face suddenly seemed to detach itself and hang in mid-air before crashing down with a terrifying roar. Directly in the way there was a telegraph pole on the top of which a Jap linesman was working. By some miracle the avalanche avoided the pole with its horrified workman as it swept past to completely block the path with thousands of tons of rock. Had we been just a few seconds earlier he would have seen an even more horrific sight as the whole work force was buried.

[*Air raids had started in 1944 not only by the B29s from China but also from Admiral 'Bull' Halsey's carriers off the coasts of the Japanese home islands. This would probably account for the numerous air raid alerts that Ted notes.*]

The first air raid in the area did much to boost our morale but no one was able to get any useful information from the Nips. As time went on the warning sirens began to sound every night, sometimes three or four times. One morning on a yasumé day we were driven to the shelters at 6 am and denied the luxury of our lie in. That same day we spent three hours in the shelter in the afternoon and had no food from 9 am to 7.30 in the evening.

These alarms were very important to us as they were tangible evidence that our people and the Americans were knocking on Nippon's door. It was a justification of our faith through all the years of captivity. Our jubilation must have shown because shortly after this the commandant made us a little speech in which he told us to change our attitude towards the Japanese workmen as we were rude, arrogant and impudent; and if we thought we were winning the war we were mistaken. Japanese victory would be snatched at the last minute. His speech heartened us considerably and gave us more assurance about allied victory than any news could have done.

During the early alerts we were doubled back to the camp, counted on the parade and bundled into the shelter, the last few men forced in with blows from rifle butts and the door closed on us. They were welcome diversions as it never occurred to the panic-stricken Japs to search us and we were able to smuggle all kinds of contraband into the camp. Buckets, which had been scarce at one time became so plentiful that each man had his own personal one. [*A great luxury,* as *'dhobi' buckets were always an important adjunct to life in RN ships*]

Once after we had doubled back to camp and Bogo was counting us, Flying Fortresses flew over the camp. It was a sight that made us proud of our American allies as three waves of nine beautiful silvery machines sailed majestically above the ineffectual puffs of gunfire. There were no fighters to oppose them; the much vaunted 'Wild Eagles' of Japan we heard so much about did not materialise.

The sight was so marvellous that we began to cheer and clap and Bogo went berserk. He ran screaming, kicking and punching everyone within reach, even those without so much as a smirk on their faces. The guards slashed at us with their rifles and bayonets to hasten us into the shelter. As one of the cockney prisoners was being pushed through the door he turned to the Nip who was using his rifle butt on him.

'Don't worry about me mate, it's you they're after!'

There were no moans about the discomfort of the shelter that day and even the most pessimistic among us began to smile. Each night as we heard the planes passing overhead I used to think of the airmen just a few thousand feet above us, a distance that meant the difference between freedom and captivity.

Prisoners all over Japan were now witnessing the effects of allied successes in the Pacific war. On 20 October 1944 the US 6th Army had landed at Leyte in the Philippines and by 17 April were established on Mindoro, Luzon and Mindanao. With the naval bases and airfields thus captured the Americans could effectively cut off what little supplies of oil and raw materials were still reaching Japan from their conquests in that direction. The US submarine fleet was actively engaged in the Inland Sea (between Japan and China) whilst B29s ranged over Formosa, the Philippines, China; even knocking out the main dock at Singapore. March saw the capture of Iwo Jima whose airfields were even closer to Japan and the first fire raids on Japanese cities (hence the fire precautions noted by Ted). The US 5th Fleet stepped up air strikes over southern Japan, including Nagasaki, to isolate Okinawa prior to the landings there on 1 April. They were to increase yet again with the softening up process for Operation OLYMPIC, the projected landings on Kyushu.

'April 1st. Beautiful Easter-like days this last week, days of nostalgia for me. More R.C.s, [*parcels*] one less than the number of men in the camp. We had a period of 14 days without R.C. then the Nips released 3 cigs, one twentieth tin of powdered milk and 3 oz of meat per man. Last night some Indos were caught stealing RC parcels [so] Bogo has stopped the whole camp smoking. I hear the amount of parcels found in the native rooms was colossal.

'One of the Yanks from Wake Island died on Friday, a poor small shrivelled little chap with a hunched back (about 43). Death due to asthma and malnutrition, [he was] in cells. Put there by Bogo for complaining of weakness and inability to work. Only a few days ago he was terribly beaten at the yard for stealing rice from the Nips.

'Impossible people these [Japanese], no work to do and yet one is beaten if caught idle. Twice this week I have caught it.

'The bugs are back in their nauseous millions; but a recent speculation of 3 bowls of rice and 3 pkts of fags for a mosquito net has proved most invaluable in making an almost bug-free citadel.

'About two thousand letters arrived yesterday and I'm looking forward to hearing from home.'

'April 15th. Carrying scrap iron for the best part of the last two weeks. The fellow in charge of us yesterday not satisfied with us carrying a full basket on a yo-yo pole made us carry some in our free hands. Practically no construction work. Every day we hear the siren which shows that somewhere not far distant is receiving attention. Days of awful humiliation these and intense longing to be away from these malicious people. They told us yesterday that Mr Roosevelt is dead. One would think that they were celebrating a major victory.

'Prisoners are beaten up every day now by the Gestapo and the army and the bosses of the various parties. At no time under the navy have the beatings reached such proportions.

'Just finished a German novel "All Quiet on the Western Front" which revealed deficiencies in my vocabulary but that by no means marred my enjoyment.

'The Japs are withholding Red Cross and using it themselves. Each day they have cakes made of butter and jam. The day before yesterday an American was caught stealing "mizo paste" from the store room and the Nips are dealing with him very effectively. This morning a whole room was punished because some of its inmates were caught stealing from the stores. What a life! What a camp! And what captors!'

After carrying the baskets of scrap iron on our yo-yo poles [*as mentioned above*] the next task was to sort the scrap metals in a floating workshop secured alongside ships at the fitting out jetty. For this job I positioned myself next to a convenient porthole through which I threw valuable non-ferrous castings overboard. As the job went on I became increasingly more daring and began to dispose of quite large castings. One afternoon as I was disposing of a valve through the port I became aware of a figure creeping up behind me. My pounding heart rose to the back of my throat and rising apprehension nearly choked me.

'Now the fishes can build ships as well!'

I turned in relief to see one of my Indonesian friends standing there. He and some of his friends decided to follow my example and in a short while a whole army was involved in this dangerous occupation.

I had already extended my sabotage since starting with nuts and bolts in the steam pipes. I always stood so that my shadow obscured the work when working with a fitter. The large lamps fitted for night work were irresistible. They burst with the report of a tight cork being drawn from a bottle when a small nut was dropped on them. Electric leads could be ruined by smashing the bulb and dropping the ends in a pool of water. Carborundum paste introduced into the oils sumps of fan and dynamo motors did little to increase their efficiency. Two ships returning from trials were found to have their bearings wiped [worn out]. The inspecting hanchos shook their heads and clicked their tongues, a characteristic indication of puzzlement and annoyance. The tins of grinding paste were also thrown over the side and eventually the Japs were reduced to making a mixture of metal polish and brick dust. Whether solely due to my efforts I never knew.

'April 22nd. Great developments these last few days. The guard room has been put outside the camp and two days ago the camp fenced off from the Nip quarters. Without a word of warning the officers were sent to another camp but before they left they gave us the impression that we are now on the last lap.

'We have had no fresh vegetables for a while; it is said that the Korean women on the island are not allowed to go to Nagasaki and everything is brought to them on the ferry. On repeated occasions they have come away with empty baskets and tear-filled eyes. It does seem there is an acute shortage of vegetables. We have returned to bread again, three diminutive rolls for dinner. No wonder my weight is eight stone five.

'Nips in better mood these days. Our boss becomes a kaigun next week so we see little of him. Remarkable the number of Nips being called up; they are getting younger and younger.'

For a long time we had been puzzled by the appearance of young Nips who congregated on the jetty to wave flags at someone similarly equipped on the ferry bound for Nagasaki. The mystery was solved by one of our Nips who, with the aid of a piece of chalk and complicated hand motions, explained that those who departed on the ferry were young Japs called to the colours and on their way to enlist.

When a young Jap became old enough for military service, he discarded his filthy working clothes and, dressed in his best, he called on all his friends to bid them farewell, taking with him a Jap flag which they all autographed. He next called on his boss and in that presence removed his cap and after much bowing by both of them, their heads bobbing up and down like floats on a fishing line, there followed a confidential chat ending with some more bows. The young man then joined his friends for the midday meal and listened to their speeches after which he doffed his cap again and bowed repeatedly to the accompaniment of three 'Banzais'. The party then made for the jetty, each carrying a small Japanese flag. Once aboard the ferry he stood at the guard rails looking sheepish and self-conscious while his friends cheered vociferously. When the ferry cast off he began waving his own flag which was answered by a wild fluttering of flags from the shore and more frenzied cheering, until the white scrap of bunting could hardly be seen on the distant boat.

When the sight of fluttering flags first aroused our curiosity it only occurred two or three times a week. But then the trickle became a flood and every ferry was laden with eager young men waving their red and white flags giving each sailing a carnival atmosphere.

We watched successive groups of schoolboys graduate through Boys Town. We saw them arrive in their new working suits and watched as their ardour cooled and they became as dirty and ragged as their seniors. Finally we saw them depart with their autographed flags.

Two of the more decent boys of our work party actually came to say goodbye before they left. The ones we detested looked sheepish as they passed us on the way to the ferry. When Pimply Face, Eric, the Bull, Attati and other more notorious of our tormentors left we watched them depart with glee and sped them on their way with a grin—and a prayer.

The overwhelming desire of every youngster was to serve in the Japanese equivalent of our Fleet Air Arm, the second choice being the navy whilst the army came a poor third.

[*At the time of Ted observing the farewells (April-June), the Japanese navy air arm were supplying the majority of the kamikaze pilots who were eagerly—and effectively—ending their short careers against the allied fleets off Okinawa.*]

The call for recruits made great inroads into the shipyard workforce. Production lagged and the young men who left were replaced by small boys and girls. Little girls were employed in gas cutting, electric welding and the decoration of the cabins in the ships. One day a little girl met a terrible end through a faulty cable at the end of which she writhed to her death. Our fellows nearby tried to save her, several of them being severely burnt in the attempt. But it was impossible to find the right switch amid the hopeless tangle of cables and gas pipes.

A particularly disagreeable task performed by some of the girls was to clear the threads on the nuts and bolts which had been discarded by the platers. These were salvaged by prisoners from pools of water and urine in the ships where the Japanese had relieved themselves. They rarely used the facilities provided.

By May 1945 the authorities decided that too much time was being wasted by prisoners returning to camp during air raids, so they made arrangements for us to remain in the yard. During one attack we were herded into a tunnel in the side of a hill and while water dripped on us from the roof we could see the bombers diving down on targets in the harbour. The guards drove us out before the all-clear had sounded and as we were being counted an unexpected burst of machine gun fire sent us all scampering back to the safety of the slimy tunnel. By the look of the planes and their intermittent appearance we concluded that they were from an aircraft carrier.

'Sunday, June 10th. [1945] Looks as if the camp will be breaking up. Signs of the dockyard ceasing to exist are becoming more evident every day. No more ships being laid down, cranes being dismantled – thank goodness. It's now 5 o'clock and we've had nothing to eat since 7 this morning because someone stole some potatoes from the garden near the galley. In the week the Nips were approached for some Red Cr. meat but the supply rating said that as there was 8 kilograms of meat in the stew they would not give any more.

'The foundry I notice is turning out thousands of small bombs, hand grenades I suppose. Another big speech given to the Nips the day before yesterday warning of the imminent invasion they fear, so I've heard.'

'June 17th. We eventually received our two meals together last Sunday at about 7.30, so we turned in feeling very comfortable. What a week this has been, very short rations; but I regard that as a very good sign.

'The Yanks have been asked to write a letter expressing their views on the question "Can bombing alone win a war?" Another good sign. It seems as though they [the Japanese] are having a tremendous drubbing and can't take it.

'Yesterday we were told the names of the fellows leaving the camp. I am stopping behind but Johnno and the Chief Mech. are going, unfortunately for me. It seems about five hundred of us have to remain here. The lads leave by next Thursday – how quiet it will be.

'Trouble in the yard due to fellows stealing tins of sardines, which are Jap emergency stores. Hope nothing comes of it. (Learnt later that the Koreans had been blamed for it.)

'Had a new job this week laying a pipe line near the sea front away from the yard. Wonderful scenery and freedom from interference by guards and police gives us almost a holiday spirit.

Yesterday I was touched by the first spontaneous demonstration of generosity I have experienced in Japan. Was working near the Koreans quarters and from a most dilapidated hovel a woman sent her little boy over laden with slices of dried sweet potato which he lavished on us.'

When I returned to my normal engineering duties I discovered that air raid shelters had been allocated to the various parties. Mine had been allocated a tunnel which pleased us as one party had to shelter in the concrete caisson that separated the two halves of the ill-fated dock while another had the pump room, both absolute deathtraps. When the men protested about the grave danger they would be in their objections were waved aside with an imperious gesture. By this time the wail of the siren had become so regular that that it was accepted as a daily routine. The Japs who had smiled and been so brave when warnings were first sounded were now as scared as we were.

'June 24th. The boys about to leave us were spared the misery of the yard for their last four days here. Unluckily it was discovered that the bakery had been broken into and about 90 buns and 500 tins of butter stolen. Rooms were searched and over 200 tins of butter were found in one Indonesian room. Meals were stopped that night and the following morning for the fellows who were leaving. In our room we had 20 rations {including short rations for two sick men] but most of the workers shared their food with the others. By dinner time the camp authorities had relented and in the evening we came back from work to normal rations.

'The boys left on Wednesday at midnight, I felt badly saying goodbye to the Chief and Johnno after having been with them since March 1941. The camp is very quiet and deserted like a vision of the future when we will all be gone. Our room has merged with the next one and there are forty three of us. Bugs this week have been especially bad [making it] quite impossible to sleep on the bunks. I tried sleeping on the table and stools but found it just as impossible. Finished up by walking up and down until Reveille. Yesterday we had the room steamed again and had a really good night's sleep. Plenty of air alerts this week, specially at night.'

Captain Farley was left in charge with the doctors, Budding and his assistant Franks, Mr Beckford, our Warrant Mechanician and the

Dutch adjutant remaining. About a thousand men were transferred to other camps leaving only five hundred of us behind. With the exodus went my great friends, Chief Mechanician Bennett and Mechanician Johnson who had nursed me so tenderly through my illness.

It was almost certain that Germany had been defeated and the Japs would never endure the bombings that both the UK and Germany had sustained. It was the popular opinion that Nippon would fold within three months.

With the exodus of two thirds of our numbers, the remaining five hundred were reorganised into different working parties. I was transferred to the pipe bending shop where the work was hard, hot and very dirty. As I had no soap at the time I felt particularly miserable but I must have made some sort of impression on the Japs because I was promoted to hancho, in which capacity I was able to create a sweeping job for myself. My assistant was Cornelius a small but spirited Dutchman and we both took advantage of ample opportunities to loaf behind the large heaps of piping in the shop. The rest of the party was badly treated, being kicked and punched around by the mere boys who worked in the shop.

The hancho of the shop was a fairly rational man who with his assistant was in charge of the whole work force, prisoners and boys. If an idle prisoner was brought before the boss he would listen to both sides of the story and if he decided in favour of the prisoner he would slap his own men about the head and face. However the veracity of the interpreter's version of events was questionable because many innocent prisoners were punished for no apparent reason. The second in command was a miserable little man, with old shoes three sizes too big, broken and down at heel. His socks had no heels to them and his legs were bound up in ridiculous puttees. His main duty was to assume responsibility for us from the police each morning and before we started work we had to salute him and he always demanded his 'kerrei' once again when we left at night.

As the number of alerts increased so did the fear of the Nips. They pulled down many wooden huts replacing them with steel structures and converting much of the space created into gardens. All stores were moved into the safety of a tunnel and fire parties were organised and exercised regularly.

By this time (mid-1945) the American incendiary raids around the main industrial areas were at their height. Owing to the impossibility of high level precision bombing the residential areas surrounding the industrial sites were set on fire (Japanese houses were made of paper and wood) which in turn destroyed the factories. The morale of the civilian population slumped rapidly because, like the German population, they had been promised victory and also assured that no enemy bombs would ever drop on their native soil. This in contrast to the 'Blood, toil, tears and sweat' promised to the British by Churchill. Ted had seen that the end was very near in the faces and attitudes of the Japanese work force, some becoming more brutal, others increasing trade and contact with the prisoners in a bid for mere survival.

I wasn't very happy when our shelter was changed from the security of a tunnel to a shallow subway built through reclaimed land. When the tide was low there was ample room for us but at high water the sea seeped through the surrounding soil into the subway which dipped in the middle and filled waist deep with water. The two ends were closed by steel doors perforated with small holes to allow some circulation of air. During an air raid we would sit four abreast on pieces of wood facing down the slope like a cinema audience. At the first warble of the siren there was a frantic race for the shelter, not because of the bombs but to get the driest seats for the session.

'July 1st. The Indonesian who went to jail 2 years ago is now again with us despite the rumour we heard about his death. From what I hear he has some wonderful news. He predicts the end by September.'

His return came as quite a shock to us and he was looking far healthier that any of us. The first three months of his confinement were spent on his knees, a favourite trick of the Nips. Later he was allowed to work on a farm which he said he enjoyed. He boasted that, on the whole he had spent a much more pleasant time than us during the same period. On his arrival back at the camp he was with the camp commandant for a couple of hours who had forbidden him to divulge any news or tell us of the sights he had seen. Which did not stop him telling us that on his journey back to the camp he saw fearful devastation in the Japanese countryside and passed through ravaged cities, which confirmed our suspicions that Nippon was catching it in the neck. He was reluctant to tell us the news but he did say that it was all over bar the shouting and we would be free by September. By this time I had become inured to optimistic reports brought in by newcomers but this news seemed to have a ring of truth about it.

By August it was obvious that Japan was fighting for survival. My party had nothing to do and yet the men had to appear busy to avoid punishment. I sought further territory to conquer with my broom and became a road sweeper. For a considerable distance around the pipe bending shop the road was maintained in an immaculate condition with the help of my Dutch assistant. Sweeping is an ideal occupation for loafers, it is so easy to appear to be busy with a broom in one's hand and we were never caught idling.

This was a great contrast to the early days when the Japs used all kinds of schemes to induce their captives to work. Rates of pay were introduced in accordance with work done, a bread bonus was given to outstanding workers, or an early finish provided that a given stint was completed, as well as riveting and drilling races between the various nationalities. They even used Red Cross supplies to reward those who worked hardest and the rooms with the least sickness. Some succumbed to these blandishments, one gang of Dutch riveters becoming so proficient that it could outdo the best Japanese gang. Some of the British were also eager to lick the hand that beat them.

When I first saw the steel plates being unloaded from the coastal vessels I wondered at the seemingly inexhaustible supplies available to the Japs. I would watch unhappily when as fast as one pile was used it was replaced by an even bigger one. But then I gradually became aware that the supply vessels' visits were becoming less frequent. Then the ships were replaced by barges heavily camouflaged with leafy boughs and armed with a couple of machine guns manned by kaiguns.

The ships built in the yard were designated as 'A' followed by a number and when they were launched little shrines were erected at the head of the docks containing offerings of fruit and vegetables and multi-coloured paper balls were pulled apart at the bows to release flocks of pigeons that circled round the ship as she was towed to the fitting out jetty. Then work on A55 was abruptly ordered to cease when she was three-quarters riveted and almost ready for launching, and it was announced that a smaller type was to be built. From that moment A55 progressively deteriorated to a rust-covered hulk until she and her predecessors, A50 to 54 who never made it to sea, were destroyed by bombs or torpedoes.

CHAPTER 7

Something Big Has Happened Today

'August 5th. Absolutely no work for us to do; but as sweepers my little Dutch confrere and I always have a broom at hand in case any inquisitive stranger puts his nose inside the workshop. Strangely enough time passes very quickly leaning on the broom and the beauty of it is we are away from the Nips on this job, which just suits me.

'Tremendously exciting week this. Monday we ran to the shelter three times during the morning. Tuesday we had an early morning session of half an hour followed by a three hour spell about noon. Wednesday we could see countless planes through the holes in the shelter door and many bombs were dropped with most actually in the yard. In the camp machine gun bullets came inboard and there were holes in the roof. Later one of the Indonesians found the nose cap of a one inch shell under his bed.

'But Thursday was easily the best day of the week. We went to shelter at 11.30 and came out at 5.30. We were in the tunnel this time and just made it with machine gun bullets spraying all around. Terrified little boys and girls [*Japanese workers*] scrambling under one's feet, Korean women with babies on their backs and clutching children by the hand, all made a terrible picture of panic and chaos. One awkward Dutchman knocked over a Korean woman with a baby twice in rapid succession. Again we listened to the crump of exploding bombs—most unmistakable. We were all pretty glad to leave the tunnel in the evening being sore with sitting down all day.

'As we emerged we saw that A53, the last ship to be finished and now lying in midstream, had been hit astern and was well down and smoking heavily. I should say that the engine room had been hit as there was a beautiful hole in the ship's side where the bomb had passed through. During the night a terrific wind sprang up and the following day she dragged her anchor, ending up on some rocks on the opposite side of the anchorage, just in front of some oil tanks – a great target for the next visit!

'Friday night we saw sailors from the ship carrying little boxes, presumably containing the ashes of their dead comrades. There were fifteen. The weather was very stormy for the following two days but by today it had cleared and now as I write allied planes are again overhead and we are standing by to go to shelter.

'We have had another food cut and it's getting serious. We only have three-quarters of a bowl of rice now. No fresh veg, for three months and no morning "stew". But I'm still confident that it's a good omen and we are on the last lap.

'How it heartens a man to hear the allied planes dive-bombing and the beautiful smooth roar of the planes engines all striving for our freedom. But what a feeling to be bombed by one's own allies after having been bombed by Jerry at home five years ago!'

'<u>August 9th 1945.</u> Something big has happened today. Something so cataclysmic that I think new forces have been unleashed on this unfortunate country now writhing in its death throes. I am fearful for our safety if there is to be a repetition of the holocaust we have just survived.

'At about eleven o'clock this morning I was sweeping the main road with my Dutch colleague, Cornelius. It was a brilliant cloudless day with scarcely a breath of wind. Everything was still, distant objects were shimmering in the heat haze and the idea of any physical exertion was repugnant—except for the guards who were more than usually active.

'Without warning there was a flash so intense that the brilliance of the summer morning was quite eclipsed. Then followed almost simultaneously a tremendous explosion and a blast of hot sickening air. The sides of the machine shop, heavy cast-iron sections, were blown across the road and all the glass in the windows left its moorings in a hail of splinters.

'I flung myself, or was flung, full length on the road with all the breath crushed from my body. Submerged in a swirling cloud of dust I lay choking and helpless and a horrible suspicion crossed my mind—chemical warfare. When I dared raise my eyes there was a vast column of ebony black smoke, shot with flames ranging from red and yellow to orange and brown rising into the air with tremendous speed. Panic gripped me. I thought, if only I could get a wet sack for my head it might help to combat the menace. Still paralysed with fear I waited for the next onslaught and the end of the world.

'The sound of running feet brought me to my senses and gave me strength to get up and make for the subway shelter. The dust and smoke was so thick as to obscure the sun and cause a twilight, as the top of the pillar of smoke now spread out like a gigantic mushroom. We were all badly scared and grimed from head to foot with a thick tenacious dust. No-one was badly injured, just a few who had been cut by glass. The odd thought crossed my mind that no-one in the shelter was grumbling about the water which was waist deep in the centre.

'As the electricity was off and there was no secondary generator on the island, there was no work for us and we loafed uncomprehendingly until five o'clock. Glancing back in the direction of Nagasaki as we walked back to camp, the smoke had settled over the town in an oily black cloud, which later in the evening was tinged with rose.'

The following morning on our way to the shipyard we watched as scores and scores of badly burnt Japanese started arriving from Nagasaki. I was horrified to see babies shockingly scorched, many of them with skin hanging in shreds from their tiny bodies. Pity welled up within me at the sight; and the thought of the inhabitants of the devastated city; the women, the children and helpless hospital patients. Many of the men looked at us with open hostility and it seemed to me that only the presence of the guards prevented them from attacking us.

We estimated that the shipyard was five miles from Nagasaki with our camp a further mile and a half away. Even at that distance nearly all the windows had been blown out and the end walls of the buildings had been bulged out by the force of the blast. The shipyard was in a ruinous state. The roads were littered with glass, buildings were in various stages of collapse and the roof of the big dock looked as if a playful giant had been busy with an enormous pair of shears. The damage would have been much more serious had it not been for two hills between the island and Nagasaki which had apparently absorbed or deflected the greater part of the blast.

None of the workmen who used to commute from Nagasaki came to the shipyard after this but there was a steady traffic of hundreds and hundreds of little wooden boxes to the city for the remains of the victims.

There followed a period of frenzied activity with blast pits being dug and the remaining glass removed from the windows. It was obvious that the Japs were bracing themselves for a last stand and also clear that release for us was near, either by the arrival of the allies or through a misdirected bomb.

For a week we did scarcely any work, most of the time being spent in the subway. There was no electricity and therefore no siren, so we scampered to the air raid shelter at the least sound of an aero engine. There we sweltered until the indefatigable corporal of the guard hounded us out on to the roadway to be counted in the broiling sun; after which, for sheer spite we were doubled away to our various places of work, with the little man running up and down the ranks like a terrier. One morning in his zeal he slipped and fell backwards all asprawl, field glasses in one direction, helmet in the other to the unconcealed amusement of everyone.

'Wednesday 15th August. Had a day off today, ostensibly the Nips are having a day of prayer; but we think that they have received warning of a three day attack. Yesterday we heard a rumour that Russia was now in the war. Another says that casualties in Nagasaki are 50,000 dead and 38,000 houses destroyed.'

'Last night we were told that we may be called to shelter during the night and to take as much of our gear as possible with us. I notice that the Japanese soldiers have adopted the same technique as most of our boys who have small bags to carry their stuff. But the brave Nippon soldiers have a rock shelter to live in while our protection consists of a few inches of earth.

'But it looks as if the climax is at hand—but which freedom I wonder? Yasumé from work today. Cleared out a drain in the forenoon. Had an alert that lasted for an hour or so, the all-clear sounding between 10 and 11 o'clock.'

When we assembled for work the following morning, the duty shuban said there was no work to be done. The guards were not wearing their steel helmets and they had also left off their puttees and were wearing shoes instead of boots.

Hopes began to rise in the afternoon when valuables were restored to those fortunate enough to have some. On the next day when Red Cross parcels were distributed hopes became a certainty that we were going to be freed. Whispers from friendly guards strengthened this belief whilst by Friday it was semi-official that hostilities had ceased on the previous Wednesday at midnight.

I wanted to believe this marvellous news and knew it was true; but there remained the niggling doubt that this might be another of the sadistic moves that the Japs liked to inflict on us. I awoke in the mornings with my mind awhirl and struggling to bring order to my thoughts as I tried to realise that freedom had arrived at last. It was a sensation very much like that I experienced as a child on Christmas

Eve, intense excitement and an unendurable pleasure in the anticipation of things to come.

'Monday August 20th.

"Both Japan and the allies stopped fighting under an agreement and truce will be signed shortly. Then the war which has lasted almost four long years will be over. We know you are tired of life in the prisoners of war camp. We imagine how happy you are now. Your cherished hopes to be with your loved ones will be fulfilled. We are not enemies now, we are friends with one another. We do not know when you start for your homeward journey. We will let you know as soon as the date is announced by the army. Until then let us have an orderly and peaceful life and we will help you that you may be able to start for home safely. On the other hand you are request-ed to keep orderly lives, observe the rules and regu-lations until then."

"Commander."

'This notice was put up today and finally settles any lingering doubts about what we guessed on Thursday last.

'On Sunday night I attended a church service in the bathroom conducted by Doctor Syred. His simple speech in conclusion, to the effect that war was a most unsatisfactory method of settling international affairs, the hymn "Abide with me" and the National Anthem all combined to move me strongly. The "King" especially brought home to me that we were no longer slaves; and although these Japs had tried to break our spirit they had merely bruised it.

'Sunday night the blackout precautions were lifted and we slept with blazing lights and open windows. The boys are smoking everywhere and the Dutch are busy refurbishing their uniforms – so we must be free!'

The Japs kept a number of pigs in the camp and they gave one to us in an effort to foster our goodwill. They first tried to kill it by battering it with a hammer but the unfortunate animal survived the assault. One of our fellows who had been a slaughterhouse man in civilian life mercifully brought the creature's sufferings to a quick and professional end. He was a tall man with startling blue eyes that one would never have associated with inflicting death, even on a fly. Another gift from the Japs was loads and loads of toilet paper and also more soap than we had seen in the previous three years.

'August 22nd. Started transcribing my shorthand notes extending over a period of nearly three years; something to occupy my mind for a time. It is curious how our positions vis-a-vis the guards have now been reversed. Practically all the Red Cross has been issued and we have never seen so much before. 2,000 tins of butter which the Nips had tried to keep in their rock shelter have been distributed.'

Within a week the positions of prisoner and guard were changed around. The Nips were now begging from the wretched creatures over which they had hitherto ridden roughshod. They crawled to us for food and clothes. Some of the more reasonable guards were rewarded, particularly 'Scabby', a cheerful man with a pock-marked face and huge purple lips. He had been with us for a long time during which he had never raised his voice. We showered him with food and gave him enough boots to last him and his family many years. There was also Inoye-san [Mr Inoye] one of the interpreters employed in the shipyard who was always kindly disposed towards us. When our need was desperate he smuggled in medicine for us. When prisoners were brought before him by the kaiguns he always listened to the prisoner's case and gave them the benefit of the doubt. I suspect that he also let out occasional tit-bits of news as well. He was overwhelmed with gifts of food, clothing and soap (a rare commodity at that time) and had to make several journeys from the camp to take it all away.

We also wrote him a testimonial to present to the occupying forces when they arrived:

> 'To Who it may concern,
>
> Mr Inoye is a bloody good man. He has been good to us all the time he has been with us. He is worth a thousand ordinary Japs. Look after him when you take over.   Signed

Here followed a long list of the names of men who had been helped by him.

'<u>August 22nd cont.</u> Musters have become perfunctory affairs and carried out in English, either by Mr Beckford or the Dutch adjutant. After a few days an astoundingly different Bogo re-appeared, creeping around with his comrades and, having expressed a fear of being reported to the Americans when they arrive, trying to ingratiate himself with us.

'About the only things that haven't recognised the armistice are the bed-bugs which are as bad as ever. They are left in undisputed possession of the huts, as everyone takes stools and tables outside to sleep on, or else make quite comfortable beds by threading blankets on to bamboo poles.

'I find it difficult to sleep at nights as the full realisation of being free hasn't yet dawned on me and is something I find hard to come to terms with. I often walk up and down in the moonlight, amid the snores of my colleagues, with my thoughts whirling round in my head. The facts of no more dockyard work, no more air raids and rushing to the shelter, no more humiliation or anxiety about food, unlimited supplies of soap and water; all are difficult to take in after so long.

'On the other hand the evidence is there and results are beginning to show. The first seven days saw a vast improvement in everybody. I could feel my strength returning and I was getting cleaner as every afternoon I disappeared in a welter of lather, rinsed away by clear water.

'The Red Cross supplies have been released and the sick bay is overwhelmed with medicines of every kind and row upon row of bandages adorn the hitherto empty shelves. We have also been issued with vitamin tablets. It is infuriating to realise that these supplies had been there all the time while men died through lack of drugs and others endured painful surgery for lack of anaesthetics that were available all the time; their wounds afterwards dressed in filthy rags while countless rolls of bandages were immediately at hand. The Nips have some awkward questions to answer when the time comes.

'<u>Monday August 27th.</u> Glorious week of freedom, the boys have been walking around all hours of the day and night smoking willy-nilly. The Nips have taken a back seat and abandoned their arms and remain outside the fence.

'The day before yesterday we were told that allied planes would be flying over the camp from 6 am onwards. Tried to sleep in the afternoon but kept running in and out as planes passed over very high. Mighty four-engined machines that scintillate beautifully in the sunshine.

'Yesterday another restriction was lifted and we were allowed to stretch our legs outside the fence. Went to church in the evening to offer my heartfelt gratitude.

'Today was our big day however. During the forenoon we heard aircraft and, dashing outside saw several four-engined machines followed by twin engined flying boats. In passing they had obviously seen our PW sign laid out on the parade ground and painted in black and yellow on the roofs. A flying boat was the first to acknowledge us with a lazy waggle of its wings, at about 11 o'clock. The four-engined bombers then returned, gradually decreasing height and finally finishing by just skimming the roofs of the camp buildings; a highly dangerous feat rendered all the more so by the surrounding hills being wreathed in mist. Today there was particularly poor visibility.

'Several cartons of "Old Gold" cigarettes were dropped and then a message was accurately planted on the roof of the sick bay, which read: "Hey boys, stand by! We are going to drop a box of rations with a message inside."

'In a few more runs boxes of rations were dropped in and around the camp, there being sufficient for us all to have a taste of real freedom food. If these are iron rations then I should have liked to starve with the allies! [*they were probably boxes of one-man 'K' rations*]

'I shall always remember "Headliner" and "Stratoliner", the names written on two of the bombers that gave us such a thrilling half hour.

'In the afternoon we had a visit from two-engined bombers, fearsome looking machines with machine guns bristling fore and aft, with a turret amidships and ghastly faces painted on their bows. They were not as daring as the big boys but after we had put the word "NEWS" on the parade ground they dropped the following in a Red Cross container:

"Courtesy of 345 Bombing Group, 500 Bombing Squadron, Air Apaches — The war is over. Japan surrendered unconditionally after Atomic Bomb dropped on Nagasaki and after Russia entered the war against Japan. MacArthur will arrive in few days time to accept Hirohito's surrender. American troops soon be here to free you."

'This is the first authentic news to reach us for three years and eight months.'

'Tuesday 28th August. Visited again by the Yanks: First came a couple of flying boats including our particular friend who spotted us.

He gave us his awkward waggle of recognition and raised a trouble-some lump in my throat. We were running in and out all day as various aircraft of all descriptions passed over. Early in the forenoon two large boxes of cigarettes were dropped in the camp by parachute; enough for two packets of twenty each. In the afternoon a bevy of fighters showed us their paces to the awe of the guards and hanchos. Later a huge four-engined plane passed over followed by another one with "PW Supplies" painted on its wings. It seems that the relief organisation is under way and just in time, as our Red Cross supplies are looking very shaky.

'Crowning example of Riceface's audacity— after taking out enough of the Red Cross supplies [for the camp's use] and selecting the most valuable items out of the remainder, he had them packed in cases on which he was going to write his name and an address in Java. However Captain Farley spiked his guns when, as senior medical officer he decreed that all medical stores be returned to the Red Cross representative with the recommendation that they be used to alleviate the suffering in Nagasaki. Riceface is now quite haughty and arrogant towards the Japs and has conveniently forgotten the days when he ran with them for cigarettes and extra rice.'

'Wednesday 29th August. Yesterday the Japs invited our officers to dinner for which several chickens and some pork had been prepared. It was not long before the saki had warmed the vitals and loosened the tongues of men not accustomed to hard liquor for many years and sounds of revelry could be heard. Several who had enjoyed permanent jobs in the camp wormed their way into the room and were soon also the worse for wear. Most of us felt the officers should have refused the invitation in the first place, particularly as, when the evening ended, someone called for three cheers for Bogo!

'A certain English petty officer has much to ponder on in this connection, as he has in all his dealings with the Japs. From the very first he volunteered to act as servant to the Nips who ran the galley, whether sergeants, corporals or privates. On this occasion when he saw the men trying to gatecrash the party he was heard to observe "If I had a rifle and bayonet, I'd keep the swine out!"

'Friday 31st August. The Dutch arranged a big day today, Queen Wilhelmina's birthday. They all mustered in the early morning and had a little ceremony involving hoisting the flag, with Riceface, looking very Prussian in his green uniform taking the salute and finally giving a speech. To follow there was to be a sports programme but our big brother aeroplane came over with bomb doors open and obvious intentions. Wilhelmina's birthday was quickly abandoned as the Dutch realised food was involved.

'The first drop was good with most of the 'chutes landing in the camp, including a direct hit on the roof of a building. Subsequent drops were wider of the mark as a slight breeze had sprung up and we all immediately left the camp in search of the missing containers. Blacky and I wandered for miles in our search just as if we were free. Smashed tins were everywhere with the Nips pinching stuff as fast as they could. Can't help feeling sorry for these poor devils now. On every occasion they're begging cigarettes and whatever else they can get from us.

'Among the supplies dropped were boots and clothing enough for 500 men.

'We've sampled tin fruit already, the burst tins having been opened and the contents distributed. Nippon says tinned food is inferior but this inferior food is the best I've tasted for three and a half years. The task of sorting the stuff is going on and planes are roaring overhead again. A Nip was killed by a cask which broke free of its parachute. Was disgusted to see the petty thieving of loose chocolate and fruit by all nationalities, especially the English. The Dutch, poor chaps are always hungry and the Indonesians are inveterate thieves anyway but for the English it's unforgivable.

'Our soup at supper was good thick yellow pea soup with plenty of body. Had a walk as far as the Nip village in the evening. Sad news from another camp where a British WO [Warrant Officer] was killed by a cask that broke from its parachute. How terrible to survive these long years of starvation and then be killed by a parcel of food.'

The second of September started off with a feeling of tension in the camp. At 10 'clock in the morning the Dutch were to be seen replacing the guards in the guard room. We had not heard a word about this and it looked at first sight as if the Dutch, on their own volition were taking charge of us. As usual it was Budding the interpreter who had kept the English speaking prisoners in ignorance and there was a great deal of anger that we had not been informed. However later in the day Captain Farley mustered us in the sick bay where he informed us that the officers had accepted the formal surrender of the Japanese staff. He went on to say:

'Beginning today you will take over guard of this camp as representatives of the allied nations until such times as formal instructions are received from the occupation forces. Beginning at a specified time we will establish our own guard in and outside the camp, supervised by our own officers and consisting alternately of British and Dutch troops.

'We have informed the Japanese that none of them will be allowed into the camp except those designated to receive orders from us regarding food, clothing and information ordered by the army of occupation.

'I ask you men to be orderly and refrain from contact with the Japanese; and remember, we are the masters now. Allow no racial prejudices to enter your feelings and remember we are the United Nations working together.'

Budding had just risen to interpret for the Dutch when a bomber flew over the camp and started dropping supplies. Owing to the danger of casks breaking loose we vacated the building rapidly and, as the drop had been scattered we spent the rest of the day searching the surrounding hills in torrential rain and clad only in shorts.

But despite our diligence there was at least a fifty per cent loss of the stuff dropped as the loads had been far too heavy for the chutes. Some of the men carried out a search in Boys Town and found a considerable number of food parcels which had been looted by the Japs. They had an enjoyable time turning the place topsy-turvy just as the Nips would have done had the situation been reversed. On one occasion whilst retrieving air drops I came across a familiar Nip figure holding one of our parcels in his hand. It was Sokato, the hancho that Johnny had promised to 'bat over the head'. I was amazed to discover how much I had come to hate these people because it gave me enormous pleasure to mete out much the same treatment that he had meted out to us.

During the search of Boys Town a grand piano was discovered and carried triumphantly back to our camp on four yo-yo poles by eight men. Installed in the sick bay its music added to the feeling of renewed life and freedom. Riceface proved to be a very competent player with good taste and almost feminine touch in contrast to his brutal surgical techniques.

For several days we experienced the heaviest rain we had ever seen in Japan. Inadequate drains choked and the whole camp was flooded, rooms and passages became knee-deep in water. Failure of the power supplies didn't help matters but we overcame this by improvising candles out of the waxed wrappings from the food parcels. We also heard the terrible news that one of the supply planes had crashed into a neighbouring hill killing the six man crew. The news depressed us because the Americans need not have risked the flight as we had enough food to last us for several weeks. We would have far rather gone without than have them die for us in that way.

Almost from the first air drop we had daily visits from every type of plane imaginable. Fighters would sweep in low over the camps at terrific speeds, giving us a wonderful sense of security although we were almost knocked off our feet by their slipstream. Our friendly flying boat never failed to acknowledge our waves with a friendly waggle of its wings. Other large planes with 'PW Supplies' painted on their wings were evidence that a massive relief operation was in action and we were completely independent of the Japanese for everything but water. The knowledge that we were being so well looked after and the rich food such as bacon, sausages, butter, cheese, dried milk and coffee contributed to a marvellous feeling of euphoria in the camp.

We soon perfected an organisation for the collection of the food parcels which the Americans literally showered on us and largely eradicated the looting by the Japs. A party of four men under a leader was assigned to each of the hills around the camp and, as soon as the parcels were located a signalman in the party semaphored to the camp and a carrying party was sent out. From my hill it was possible to see another camp farther down the harbour being supplied in like manner. The packages weighed about forty pounds each and contained sufficient food for ten men for one day. Each parcel invariably contained a message or a request to write to the airmen when we got home. One message read; 'Gentlemen we are glad to be with you again. These are missions we do enjoy.'

'September 8th. We can now walk outside the camp anywhere on the island and practically unmolested. The Jap military police appear friendly and have only once turned us back from an AA battery. I went for a walk yesterday and found that apart from the road between the camp and the shipyard there are only rough paths on the island. The scenery is very beautiful and from the top of the hills one can see little islands standing out like green jewels in a brilliant blue sea. Our camp looks surprisingly substantial from the high ground above it and better that the Japanese dwellings.

'We now have a short wave radio and the boys are watchkeeping in an endeavour to to find out the times of news broadcasts. The night before last I was shaken [*woken up*] at 2.30 in the morning to take down a news broadcast in shorthand but I arrived at the tail end of it.

Last night there was a particularly clear news from Aussie at about 6.30 pm and I managed to get it all down but it took me until gone nine o'clock to transcribe it. With items taken from the digests dropped with our supplies and coupled with the Dutch news we circulate quite a useful daily news sheet, typed on the typewriters we have managed to acquire.

'Yesterday evening we were visited by an American press correspondent of a Chicago newspaper. He's had a very exciting time in the war having escaped from Java. He wouldn't listen to the Dutchmen's experiences, all he wanted to cover was the *Exeter's* last action. He also told us we now have a Labour government which collared eighty per cent of the electorate in the recent election.

'We have a lot of visitors from other camps and it seems this sort of thing is happening all over Japan with ex-prisoners wandering about at will. Fortunately they don't stay long as they pass through Nagasaki on the way where typhus is rife.'

The days passed fairly rapidly at this time. Transcribing my diary into longhand was quite a task as there was a huge accumulation extending over a period of four years. The hours spent doing this would be interspersed with gathering supplies from the air drops, a bath in the afternoon and the evening meal. Mostly we passed the time in a holiday atmosphere of sunbathing and swimming or making rafts which we paddled across the bay. We also made friends with dozens of little boys and girls obviously evacuated from Nagasaki. We joined in their games and swam races with them. They contributed enormously to our happiness and rehabilitation to the humane world we had lost. We gave them more chocolate and food than they had ever seen in their lives and if possible they were even happier than we were.

During one of my walks around the island I called at the dockyard hospital and, in the course of a conversation with a Japanese doctor I learned that people were still dying as a result of the atomic bomb. He had recently failed to save the life of his niece from a strange malady which he was unable to diagnose and from which many of his patients were suffering. He was completely baffled by this illness and was helpless in dealing with it. He estimated that the death roll was 90,000 and the number of houses destroyed was 38,000. It seemed terrible that a single bomb in one blast could incinerate so many victims and afterwards go on killing those who survived with a slow and lingering death. I felt strongly for

Liberation 1945. Part of *Exeter*'s ship's company from Macassar. (IWM)

the doctor and his patients and the hatred I felt for the Nips was greatly diminished after my visit to the hospital.

On 9th September American ships could be seen lying off the the entrance of the harbour and for a few days after the air was filled with the sound of explosions which we guessed were mines being detonated. One day while we were on the shore a minesweeper came so close that one of our signalmen semaphored a message asking for us to be taken aboard. The message was acknowledged and the reply spelt out: 'Sorry boys, we have a job elsewhere.'

On 11th I was chosen to represent the Britishers in the camp at a combined memorial service for the Americans who had been killed on their mercy mission to us and for those of us who had died in the camp. We carried the stretcher bearing the caskets containing the ashes of the airmen, covered with the Stars and Stripes, from the camp down to the ferry and to the church at Nagasaki. The service which I believe was Roman Catholic was in Japanese, after which the headman's son made a speech which was interpreted by the woman who superintended the female labour in the dockyard. He said that everyone was glad the war was over and that we should care for the families of those who died in Japan. He also said that Japan, with the help of other nations would rebuild the world.

The church was situated on the outskirts of the town and had escaped the major force of the blast but in spite of that the area had suffered major damage. Scores of houses were demolished and hundreds more had their roofs dangerously askew. The local inhabitants were hostile and it was a relief to get back to the camp away from them; but also from the sight of the devastation.

That same evening an American landing craft came into our little bay to take away two of our number, Jimmy Green and a Dutchman, who were dying of tuberculosis. It was rumoured that they were going to fly Jimmy home to spend his last days with his family.

CHAPTER 8

Homeward bound

'<u>September 12th.</u> There was an unfamiliar roar of engines in our little bay this afternoon and on dashing out to investigate we found that we had been invaded by American landing craft. They brought with them Commodore Wilcon USN and the captain of the US Hospital Ship *Haven*. As the commodore passed us we saluted and he said "We'll be moving you tomorrow morning, boys!" and to the accompaniment of loud cheers went on to say that every effort would be made to get us home as quickly as possible.'

That was the last entry in my prison diary. Within half an hour of Commodore Wilcon's arrival United States 'Recovery Teams' went into action. We were handed printed forms to be filled in and we were examined by American doctors. Their sympathy and tenderness were extremely moving and something we had been quite unused to for a long time. They stared aghast at the scars and deformities perpetrated by the butcher on our men. The sergeant in charge of recovery asked people who had kept diaries to submit them for inspection as they might reveal information regarding the ill-treatment of prisoners and names of the perpetrators. Reluctantly I handed mine in, in the hope it would be of some help. All that afternoon gum-chewing American sailors roamed all over the camp taking shots of the camp with cine cameras.

September 13th 1945 was like the end of term but multiplied a thousand times. Everyone was up by five o'clock and after breakfast our last meal in the camp we tipped up the stools and table and smashed all the crockery for which the Japs had been charging us for all the time we had been there. Then between eight and nine o'clock there came once more the sound of engines as the Americans returned to take us away. The tiny bay was filled with landing craft and as we walked down to the seafront the entire village, including many of our former guards turned out to watch us go. There were also our small playmates of the last few days, some in tears as we waved them goodbye. Before I went I took one last look around what had been our home. Despite starvation, disease and death, the camp had been a refuge from the snow, wind and rain, and also from the dockyard with its attendant savagery of beatings and fearful working conditions. Now its outlook had completely changed. The one time menacing machine gun pits were holes filled with muddy water, the air raid shelters that we had built and in which we had spent so much time were in a state of collapse. The buildings had holes in the roofs where shingles had long ago been dislodged and not replaced; smashed windows added to the air of desolation. A sudden feeling of revulsion came over me as I turned away. Had we really managed to survive for three years in such a dreadful place?

The trip to Nagasaki was very quick and we landed in front of the American hospital ship *Haven* who towered above us like a snow white palace. On the jetty nurses in civilian clothes who took down our details were the first white women we had seen for nearly four years and their sympathy and understanding raised a lump in my throat. One of the things I noticed was that painted finger nails were still the fashion but even without such aids they were the most beautiful beings I had ever seen.

While we waited our turn to be interrogated we were given coffee and doughnuts as a sort of introduction to the luxuries to follow. As I drank my coffee, a squad of Nips passed by with picks and shovels on their shoulders, under the charge of a youthful American sergeant, whilst in the background could be seen the awful evidence of the atomic blast. Whole sides of what had been green mountains were scorched black, whilst in the town remnants of melted steel girders stood out like partly burnt candles. The town itself was entirely destroyed, just a huge plain of rubble. It was a horrifying sight.

On board the hospital ship we stripped off our filthy clothes and luxuriated in hot and cold showers with abundance of clean water and masses of fragrant lather. We were then dusted from head to foot with a white powder and sprayed making me feel just as a newly bathed and dusted baby might feel. We then collected our personal effects —also sprayed and disinfected. After a medical inspection we went to a dressing room having collected on the way a pair of shorts, a vest, socks, trousers, slippers, shirt and a belt. As we dressed the transformation from dirt and filth to clean bodies, new clothes, no itchiness or discomfort and the vague awareness of the fragrance of soap was indescribable. It seemed a marvellous dream from which I dreaded being woken up to find myself back in camp. Returning to the jetty a nurse presented me with a New Testament and, when sufficient numbers had gathered to make a boatload we were whisked away to the American aircraft carrier *Chenango* to start the first leg of our journey home. The crew treated us immediately with great kindness amid a great deal of curiosity on either side.

The midday meal which had been prepared for us was collected from a servery on metal trays with compartments which were filled by the servers. Everything was unbelievably good but what I enjoyed the most was the bread—snow-white and pure and wholesome. It seemed that everything was available and one only had to ask for anything one fancied.

A film show was put on for us in the evening but I was quite content to pace the flight deck alone to get some sort of order into the chaotic state of my mind. It was hard to get used to integrating with other people outside our closed community. The swift turn of events, new faces new voices, new conversation, the absence of Nips, vermin, hunger and disease was very bewildering and difficult to take in. Everything that made up the normal world and had been absent for so long in our lives was novel and exciting. Using a real lavatory and sleeping on a camp bed were luxuries. Smooth cheeks and chin after shaving with a real razor instead of a sharpened kitchen knife; using nail clippers instead of tearing one's finger and toe nails to keep them under control. To be able to lie down and rest huge legs swollen with beriberi and not think of fleas and bugs. It was all nearly too much to take in.

Whilst I was strolling up and down the flight deck I noticed a Japanese steamboat about to cross our bows which was contrary to regulations. A few rounds of machine gun fire made it change direction in a hurry. Somehow this incident gave me great pleasure and it was good to see the Nips taking orders after they had humiliated us for so long.

After embarking many hundreds more ex-prisoners we left next morning under a pleasing sky of mother of pearl, grey-blue and rose. Our ship slipped by the Mitsubishi yard in the wake of a prim little destroyer whose stern rose and sank in rhythm with our snub bows. Numerous minesweepers were still at work in all the bays and inlets. We passed the *Chenango*'s sister ship *Suwannee*, impressive with her fighters ranged on the flight deck.

I tried to locate the camp but a projecting point hid the view. In the dockyard ship A54 was still alongside the fitting out jetty, deserted and rusting and not a soul to be seen in the whole yard. The last I saw of our work place was the mangled roof of the new dock, so new and proud when we first saw it but now completely in ruins.

Gradually the island itself became an indistinct grey cloud on the horizon and Nagasaki together with Fukuoka Camp No. 2, Koyaki Jima became imperceptibly absorbed into the blue haze of the horizon.

The journey home took 47 days by ship, plane, train and ship again. Our first stop was Okinawa where we arrived on the 18th September having been through a typhoon that made the ship do everything but stand on its head. In the night a portable pump broke clear of its lashings in the hangar where we were sleeping and we had to evacuate the area hurriedly. However the duty watch quickly secured it once again and we were able to resume our broken slumbers. Inshore on Okinawa long lines of flying spray showed the presence of reefs in the otherwise green sea. After we had anchored and had our midday meal landing barges came alongside to take us ashore. The swell was alarming, the barges rose and fell as much as thirty feet and we had to jump on to the barge as it rose on the crest of a wave. I was very sorry indeed to watch a one-legged American attempting to get on board a barge. He was finally persuaded to abandon his efforts and the look on his face was pitiful.

We were taken to a camp by lorries which passed through scenes of the recent fighting with knocked out tanks and ruined buildings. But in all directions never-ending streams of lorries passed ant-like over temporary roads. Everywhere there was feverish activity, pipes were being laid roads built and land levelled by enormous machines the like of which I had never seen. They moved huge mounds of earth as if they were hills of sawdust. Around the camp there were gangs of Japanese cleaning lavatories, emptying refuse bins and doing other general tasks. They did not appear to be overworked and their tasks were very much easier and more congenial than ours had been.

The camp consisted of tents, mess halls and wash places and a Red Cross hut that supplied us with everything from newspapers, chocolates and toilet gear down to the ubiquitous Coca-Cola. There was an evening cinema show which showed shots of the fighting on Okinawa. It was difficult to concentrate on the film as there was so much going on. I was distracted by the beautiful barmy night and the fireflies and the distant lights of the lorries sweeping round the curve of the bay. Also my natural padding had not yet returned and the hard seat was uncomfortable for any length of time.

The next stage of our journey was to the Philippines by air. We were called early in the morning and taken by truck to the airfield where numbers of huge four engined B24s were warming up. Their propellers generated gales of wind that scattered litter and gravel in all directions. Those who wished to have them were given Mae West lifebelts and parachutes. The crew didn't seem particularly interested in parachutes but taking no chances at this stage, I grabbed one just in case.

On board the plane we had to sit on wooden planks fitted in the bomb bays. The bottom of the plane gaped open and as we waited to go our legs dangled into space. Dr. Syred thought we were to travel like this and the look on his face as the bomb bay doors clicked shut just before take-off was a study in relief.

The crew was amazingly young. No one objected to being addressed as 'yobs' by a boyish sergeant in charge of us. It sounded much better than the names the Japs had called us. The machine guns were still mounted in the bows, amidships and astern each with their cartridge belts in position and ready for use.

Sometimes the plane would lurch drunkenly and drop alarmingly as much as fifty feet due, as the sergeant explained, to air pockets. But we still pulled our parachutes a little closer to hand. The hard seat was very uncomfortable so I climbed into the main body of the plane and made a bed from a pile of parachutes in an unoccupied space. I was soon lulled to sleep by the hum of the engines, only returning to full consciousness when we were over Luzon. As we reached Manila we had to circle for some time waiting our turn to land. Looking out of a port I could see below me an awful shambles of what must have been a beautiful city. The houses were just shattered walls interspersed with temporary buildings of corrugated iron sheets most of which were red with rust. The area around the town was littered with the wreckage of hundreds of planes, all bearing the dull red roundel of Japan. Contrastingly parked by the airfield were neat rows of American planes.

Having circled around for an hour and a half we finally touched down; and after the seven hour flight the squeal of the tyres on the tarmac like music to our ears. As we left the plane we were greeted by a military band playing a Sousa march which was all very rousing and made us feel quite the returning heroes.

At the 'Recovered Personnel' building we feasted once again on doughnuts and coffee while smokers were given a generous allowance of cigarettes. A lorry then transported us to an extensive camp set in a sea of mud where we came under the supervision of the Australian army. For the first time since our release we were allowed to send a telegram home which said; 'Safe in Australian hands'. Each man was given a mess kit and a blanket and an extraordinary pile of miscellaneous equipment including a water bottle, a pistol belt, a pair of gaiters and a poncho, for which, with the possible exception of the poncho we had not the slightest conceivable use.

The next day after a physical examination I found that I had gained weight since leaving Japan, my chest had shrunk by four inches and I was one inch shorter. The doctor was not unduly alarmed at my condition and said my teeth and vision were in good shape anyway. He told me that a month or so on a normal diet would be all the treatment I required.

The first thing we noticed were the Japanese prisoners working around the camp, enjoying the same rations as everyone else and, we noted, a yasumé of ten minutes in every hour.

From the American papers we first learned of conditions in Britain. They painted a dismal picture of life there as a mere existence with the rationing of food, clothes and fuel and a prediction of a severe winter to come with stocks of coal drastically low. We read in the magazine 'Time' how poorly the Americans thought of us as very junior partners in the Anglo-American alliance and there was no great enthusiasm for our new Labour Government under Mr Attlee. It was all very depressing and a few took it so badly they were reluctant to go home. But it made little difference to most of us. Nothing could be as bad as the life we had just left and at least we would be sharing any misfortune with our own people. From unknown sources came various bits of news the most interesting being that Riceface had been arrested and that Harelip [*the Indonesian bugler/informer*] had been shot by the Dutch.

We spent three days in this camp during most of which it rained in torrents. The whole place was transformed into a morass and no matter where one went the mud came up over one's ankles. About the only thing to do was to lie on our beds and doze and daydream. A welcome diversion was an interrogation which occupied us for nearly an hour and there was also an open air cinema where the audience sat in the rain, either with their ponchos on or else stripped to the waist. The beer queue wasn't put off by the rain either as it shuffled forward through the mire to get a ration.

From Manila we travelled to Pearl Harbour in the new British carrier HMS *Implacable*, the first real piece of England that we had seen with the White Ensign and the Union Jack flying from her mast. From the moment we went aboard it was comforting to see the

HMS Implacable. 'The first bit of England we saw.' (IWM)

officer of the watch with his telescope tucked under his arm, the hum of auxiliary machinery and the familiar pipes over the Ship's Radio Extension and English food. For the first time it felt that we were really on our way home.

The Royal Navy personnel among the passengers were separated from the rest and also issued with uniforms so that we felt that we were once again part of the service. I introduced myself to the occupants of the mess I would have been in, had I been part of the ship's company. There were a number of Plymothians among them and they told me about the devastation in the city. Many of the landmarks, shops and cinemas that I used to go to were now gone which was very sad to hear. We also learned all sorts of new words and phrases that were completely alien to us. D-Day, VE-Day, VJ-Day, jet propulsion, radar, sonar, Jeeps, spivs, buzz bombs and V2s; all the developments in both the service and civilian world that had passed us by in our prison life.

While the ship's company existed on normal fare such as corned beef, boiled potatoes and peas we were given a special diet to build us up and as time went on we began to look more like normal human beings. Our faces filled out and the wild and staring look of sunken eyes faded. Old ingrained habits died hard however and many ex-prisoners could not get used to the idea that their next meal was assured. When for example biscuits were being issued many of the ex-prisoners would take handfuls of them. They were eating just for the sake of it. I also still found it hard to believe that I was free.

One peculiar event was recorded by me in my diary which I had started again:

'October 3rd. Still homeward bound. What a marvellous feeling. I am still not sure whether this is a dream. Please God let it be true, if all were a dream I should be devastated.'

'October 3rd. What's this? Another Wednesday? An odd week this, eight tots of rum in seven days. Will we get eight days pay, I wonder?'

We had of course crossed the international dateline with the extraordinary pipe over the SRE 'Today is no day. Tomorrow is Wednesday.'

Next day we arrived at Pearl Harbour where we refuelled for the next stage to Vancouver. After being used for so long to a complete blackout, the sight of the harbour all lit up seemed ultra-brilliant. All the ships had crimson lights at their mast heads. There were numerous varicoloured signal lamps, revolving lights on control towers and the navigating lights of aircraft flying overhead seemed like jewels against the night sky.

On October 6th we arrived at Vancouver where every ship welcomed us with their sirens and whistles. Thousands of cheering spectators watched us pass under the graceful suspension bridge and secure alongside. After we had been paid in Canadian dollars we disembarked; the naval contingent being the first to leave the ship. Each man was cheered as he walked down the gangway and along the road to a waiting train, where Red Cross girls were distributing fruit, chocolates and cigarettes. The British Columbian apples were wonderful and as I bit through the hard crimson skin to the crisp pink-tinged flesh it came to me that this was one of the things I had missed most. It seemed the whole population of Vancouver was gathered at the station to speed us on our way. The warmth of their send-off was overwhelming.

On the way to the Rockies, dimly seen in the distance, the train took us through the changing scenery of grazing lands and cattle, farm houses and an occasional little church. Then on to wooded land and huge expanses of muddy water, with here and there a sawmill almost hidden by huge piles of sawdust. The train began to climb and as the once distant Rockies loomed nearer and nearer mountain torrents surged down through the wooded hillsides. Gradually the hills became forested mountains coloured with the gold, crimson and green of autumn.

Coffee, doughnuts, soft drinks and ice cream awaited us at Calgary, with the Red Cross and Salvation Army most attentive to our needs. The hospitality was still a bit much for me and I worriedly wrote in my diary: 'What has prison life done to me? I have become almost bitter and all this hospitality and kindness seems grossly exaggerated and unnecessary.'

The novelty of eating and sleeping on a train soon became a matter of routine but at each station we would evade the military police and descend on the nearby shops to buy silk stockings, cosmetics and non-perishable foodstuffs to take home with us. Beer was in great demand but with the Canadian licensing laws alcohol had to be consumed on the premises. Because I was still reluctant to contact people I would stretch my legs in some remote part of the station. Some of our number strayed too far and missed the train. My bunkmate was one of these so I was able to use his bedding as the weather was getting colder the further east we journeyed.

On October 16th we left the train at a tiny village called Debert which was about seventy miles from Halifax. A lorry took us to a former RAF camp where pilots were trained. We were housed in comfortable, centrally heated quarters with bunk beds and four men to a room. There was an unlimited supply of hot water so I immediately scrubbed away the five days and six nights accumulation of grime from the train and, true to naval tradition I got my dhobeying up to date.

The mess room was well furnished and with a good supply of papers and magazines; and a radio that gave us BBC programmes so that we suddenly felt that we were nearly home. That evening the duty RSM declared drinks on the house and celebrations increased as the evening wore on. We sang songs and impromptu turns were given by the most unlikely people imaginable. Eventually when all the songs in our repertoire and the beer had both been exhausted we staggered off to bed. It was a long time since I had felt so happy and I was hoarse with joining in all the songs.

Time passed quickly in this camp. There were cinema shows every evening, the radio to listen to and there were always interesting discussions in progress.

On the Sunday the people of the nearby town of Truro placed their cars at our disposal to take us out. One particularly kind man drove us to the little town of Pictou where the inhabitants gave us a warm welcome. They treated us as heroes instead of prisoners of war who had been unable to take part in the fighting. Our driver was very entertaining, his dearest wish being that one day there would be a British heavyweight boxing champion of the world. All Canada seemed pleased to see us and anxious that we should stay, for on the very next day we attended a talk given by Nova Scotia emigration authorities who were extraordinarily keen for us to return to Canada after we had been demobbed.

I was by now getting more used to having people around me because one evening I had just decided to have an early night when a Canadian air force sergeant and a friend came and sat next to me and started up a conversation. To be sociable I had a glass of beer with them and before long others had joined us and a first class discussion on religion emerged from the initial small talk. My father had always warned me never to argue about religion, politics or the speed of ships, but as the evening wore on and our table became loaded with empty bottles and glasses we became more amiable, until at 2.30 am I left the mess just as the sergeant was trying to sing 'That was a cute little rhyme, sing us another one, do!'

On our last night we decided to have a great celebration in the camp. All went well until the supply of beer was exhausted. But our hosts, determined to make us drunk arranged for us to visit another mess a short distance down the road. Here we found festivities proceeding at a furious pace. A dance was in progress and every guest, before he was allowed near the bar had to have at least one dance with a charming Canadian girl. It was a very enjoyable evening; the company was congenial and the girls made us particularly welcome, doing everything in their power to entertain us and leaving us little time for serious drinking. Once again I was astounded by the warmth of Canadian hospitality. I was also grateful to them because I made many friends, I wasn't overwhelmed and I was fast losing my inability to meet strange people.

On Wednesday 24th October we left the camp in pouring rain for Halifax, stopping on the way at the town of Truro where once again Red Cross girls presented us with chocolate, cigarettes and fruit. Late that evening we boarded the French liner *Ile de France* which, like the Cunarders *Queen Mary* and *Queen Elizabeth,* had been used as a fast troopship during the war. Although we were eager to get home we also felt sorry to be leaving Canada whose citizens had given us such a warm welcome back to civilisation. Some of the fellows were leaving sweethearts whilst a few had actually got married during our short stay. The authorities, eager for British immigrants, had back-dated marriage licences so that the prospective bridegrooms would qualify for the necessary residential period.

With four thousand of us on board the ship was overcrowded. There was also no organisation to allot cabins and we were at first bundled from one compartment to another until finally in exasperation we found our selves an empty cabin. We had just settled down for the night when a crowd of Hong-Kong volunteers burst in and tried unsuccessfully to order us out. Having turned in for the night we were not moving for anyone and so the volunteers moved off elsewhere.

Since leaving Japan we had become fastidious in our cleanliness because we found the bed linen was filthy and had obviously not been changed for some time. In the camp I had never once washed my blankets, believing that the dirt would help keep me warm and now I was complaining about soiled sheets and pillows.

I still found it difficult to settle down into a normal existence and obviously my experiences still affected me. I spent most of the time walking on the upper deck away from the crowds and I felt reassured by the fact that our cabin was just below the upper deck in case anything should happen to the ship. At first with the ship being so steady in calmer seas, I would wake up in the night trying to determine whether I was on a plane, a train or a ship or even back in camp.

During the journey the overcrowding was considerably eased by the worsening of the weather. Most of the soldiers were seasick stayed in their cabins while in the mess hall the queues for food thinned out considerably and we ate our meals in some comfort. As we journeyed east the BBC broadcasts became more and more distinct. The first time we heard the nine o'clock news plainly was at six o'clock ship's time and with the clocks being advanced an hour each day, our progress was marked by the news getting nearer to its proper time.

The sea was quite calm for our last night on board and the deck was dry and level when I had my nightly stroll. The 9 o'clock news at 8 o' clock told us there was one day to go; and also of the dockers strike in Britain which appalled us. We decided to unload our own baggage if necessary when we got to Southampton. Then next morning I was on deck early to see the Scilly Isles as they came into sight over the horizon. It was 30th October, my thirty-fifth birthday and my first glimpse of England for nearly five years. The ship altered course to bring us nearer the familiar rocky coast of Cornwall and shortly after noon we passed the Eddystone light with the stump of Smeaton's lighthouse plainly visible. Plymouth loomed in the distance and, with the excitement of being so near home, I felt I could almost swim to the Hoe where the rest of Smeaton's tower stood.

We arrived in Southampton Water at nine pm and dropped anchor until the following morning. During the night the disembarkation staff came on board to give us ration cards, leave forms and travel warrants so that we could leave in the morning with minimum delay. It was 3 am when I got to bed as I had been one of the last in the queue for these formalities but I was up again at 5.30, scarcely noticing the lack of sleep. Not that I could have slept much anyway as I was in constant fear of missing some important announcement or of being left behind.

In the morning we nosed gently through a thick fog until we could see the jetty, each vessel that we passed giving us a noisy welcoming blast on her siren. One old boat lacking a siren, clanged away on a large rusty piece of boiler plate. As we made fast alongside the *Queen Mary* there were thousands of cheering people on the jetty with a brass band playing away and even occasionally being heard above the clamour.

The Naval party was the first to disembark and we were driven by coach to a naval depot, HMS *Shrapnel* where, after a perfunctory medical we were passed on once again to the Red Cross who presented us with various articles of clothing. We were then paid and given an issue of cigarettes sufficient to last the seventy days leave, which made me wonder about Customs and my kitbag full of cigarettes. Having heard there was a shortage in Britain I had accumulated them in Canada as well as nylons and underwear for the womenfolk.

Then after a midday meal we were taken to Southampton station where there was a through train to Plymouth and six of us, all Plymothians, settled down in a carriage to enjoy – or was it endure – the last part of our journey home.

During the journey the English countryside rolled past us. Green valleys, autumn ploughed fields, rivers and streams, smoke from cottage chimneys and the increasing twinkle of lights as dusk fell. The realities of what had been dreams for the last five years. There was little conversation as we watched the changing scenery. We were all preoccupied with our hopes and fears for the future and preparing for the moment of meeting our families again. I hadn't told anyone of my home-coming as I wanted to surprise everyone and also avoid a platform reunion. A private moment for the family alone.

With such thoughts we drew into North Road Station to a sea of strained expectant faces eagerly scanning each window as the train slowly came to a halt. Then the carriage doors opened and almost immediately I saw one of our number meet his wife with such happiness and joy it was overwhelming for me let alone him. Others pushed through the crowd calling a name, oblivious of anything else except the face they recognised. Soon the platform was filled with hugging kissing people, many in tears others laughing, young children greeting fathers they didn't know; mothers and wives standing back to cast a critical eye over a still gaunt frame, making a mental note to get it filled out again. Young Sammy's father was there sobbing as he greeted the son he had once thought lost.

Eventually when the initial excitement had died down, Sammy invited me to share their taxi as they lived not far from my home. This I was glad to do and they dropped me at the top of our road and in less than two minutes I was home.

I could never forget the look of relief and joy in my mother's eyes as I walked into our lounge. The signs of anxiety and strain of the last five years of war and uncertainty showed in her face and she seemed to have grown smaller. As I put my arms around her the pent-up emotions experienced in the journey from Southampton were released and I cried, like Sammy and his father in the station. Dad was much the same as he had ever been, phlegmatic but happy to see me; and relieved that all the assurances demanded of him by my mother concerning lack of news home were no longer necessary.

When later in the evening Thyra and my sister Edie came home, their happiness and tears made me realise what a strain had been put on them all. The Japs had been quick to tell of the sinking of *Exeter* but much less willing to publish news of the survivors. It was apparently twelve months before the people at home were told that some of us at least were still alive. For Edie this was the second reunion of its kind for, her husband, Russell, had been a survivor when the cruiser *Hermione* was sunk. She had recently become a proud mother and presented me with a small bundle called Diane to hold, which was about the only thing that didn't appreciate my homecoming, as she wailed a protest at my ineptitude as an uncle.

Sleeping in my own bed in my own room again was marvellous but there was a vague feeling of unreality about it. Although I slept well I was conscious of the luxury and comfort, softness and cleanliness of it all. As I lay in the half wakefulness of early morning I expected to hear the bugle calls and shouts that had been the reality of life for so long.

I explored the house from top to bottom, seeing on all sides familiar objects, each with its own particular link with the past. My books were as I had left them on the shelf, old friends that I leafed through in a new light, having learnt their true value since I last handled them. The steam engine which my father had given me over twenty years before was on its shelf, the flywheel spinning smoothly at a touch. The moths had been at my clothes in the wardrobe, my favourite plus-fours were in tatters while pullovers and cardigans were ruined. My tools were still in the outhouse and on a hook was my haversack where I had hung it after my last weekend camp. Under the table was the little stool into which I used to hammer tin-tacks when I was small.

After some hesitation I ventured outside the house and, keeping off the main streets I carried out a little surreptitious exploring. It was still not easy to walk around on my own or to meet people. Those that

I met were considerate and didn't ask too many questions for which I was grateful. Our part of St Budeaux had not been too heavily bombed although some of the familiar landmarks had gone and there were gaps in the houses like missing teeth.

As time went on I felt an improvement in my self-confidence and the human dignity which the Japs had almost destroyed returned. I felt more like a man than the creature I had been reduced to. All around me were real things, not a travesty of the genuine article. Shoes were shoes not things of rubber and cloth, clothes were made of real cloth not hessian and underpants no longer a G-string of coarse cloth. At first the most trivial things had to be looked at, felt and wondered at; but gradually I came to accept them as part of my normal life and not undreamt of luxuries as they were just a few weeks back.

With this return of confidence I was able to meet friends and talk to strangers and become a member of society once again.

From time to time I heard various items of news about the people from the past. Hookworm, a parasite picked up through walking bare footed in the camps, permanently ruined the health of many of my friends, in some cases causing death. One of my close friends, a fervent supporter of the ship's rugby XV tried to strangle his wife, then shortly afterwards died himself. It made me wonder how many more ex-prisoners of war suffered mentally as a result of their treatment in the hands of the Japanese.

During one of my visits to my local doctor he handed me a copy of The Lancet.

'Wasn't that your doctor in the prison camp?'

I nodded as words failed me at that moment. Doctor Syred had been a valued friend whose friendship and counsel had helped me and many others retain a hold on sanity during particularly trying times. With precious little else except his own personality and determination he had cured countless sick men whilst the Japs did little to help and withheld much of the medical supplies.

My friend Bandy [*Bandmaster Vidler*] from whom I was parted when I left Macassar, died in a camp in the tropics, as did Tommy the young Welshman. On the other hand, Smithy, one of my cubicle mates at Macassar, returned home and became a successful businessman. The young seaman who had been so terribly mutilated by the Jap surgeon found happiness in marrying a widow with a ready-made family of two daughters.

When the villains of our camp appeared before the war crimes tribunal they were made to pay the price for their brutality but with the judges being remarkably lenient. Flip, the galley hancho, was sentenced to twelve years imprisonment. Sumioka Harutaro the interpreter, nicknamed Beethoven, received ten years. The sergeant who worked in the office, Muria Masaaki (Napoleon) got nine years, while Yasutsako Hideo, our beloved Bo-go-go was sentenced to eight years; a ridiculous price to pay for his reign of misery and oppression. It is certain that their lot as prisoners would be far more comfortable than that of the unfortunates whom they had beaten, broken and stripped of all human dignity.

Thyra, my fiancee of six weeks when I left her in 1941, who had waited so long and loyally throughout the years of uncertainty became my wife and in 19th December 1948 presented me with twins, a boy and a girl. Thus thankfully disproving the forebodings of those who predicted that the various injections we were given in Japan would make us sterile.

For several months after my arrival home there was no news of my diary which had meant so much to me in Japan, so I wrote to the United States Ambassador in London, Mr John G. Wynant. To my great delight I received a most courteous letter from him by return and within a few days the diary was returned. As I looked through the yellowing pages I thought of all the heart-stopping moments it had caused me during countless searches it had been through. And how my friends had risked terrible beatings to keep me supplied with items of news, stub-ends of pencil and pieces of paper. In transcribing the shorthand notes from the fading paper my hatred of the Japs came to the fore again as I realised that although we lost comparatively few men in the actions at sea, over half our ship's company died as a result of their treatment by the Japanese in the various prisoner of war camps.

Bibliography

Lord Russell of Liverpool: Knights of Bushido (*Cassell,* 1958)

Gray, Edwin: Operation Pacific (*Leo Cooper,* 1990)

Johns/Kelly: No Surrender (*Harrap,* 1969)

Vat, Dan van der: The Pacific Campaign (*Hodder,* 1992)

With acknowledgements to the Imperial War Museum
and Mrs Thyra Anderson for the use of photographs
as indicated.